Choosing a Dog

An Owner's Guide To

A HAPPY HEALTHY PET

Howell Book House

IDG Books Worldwide, Inc.
An International Data Group Company
Foster City, CA • Chicago, IL • Indianapolis, IN • New York, NY

Howell Book House
IDG Books Worldwide, Inc.
An International Data Group Company
919 E. Hillsdale Boulevard,
Suite 400
Foster City, CA 94404

For general information on IDG Books Worldwide's books in the U.S., please call our
Consumer Customer Service department at 800-762-2974. For reseller information,
including discounts and premium sales, please call our Reseller Customer Service
department at 800-434-3422.

Library of Congress Catalog Control Number: 00-105671

ISBN   1-58245-059-5

Manufactured in the United States of America
10 9 8 7 6 5 4 3 2 1

Series Director: Susanna Thomas
Book Design by Michele Laseau
Cover Design by Iris Jeromnimon
Illustrations by Jeff Yesh
Photography:
  Front and back covers by Winter/Churchill/DOGPHOTO.COM
  All photography by Winter/Churchill/DOGPHOTO.COM unless otherwise noted.
    Mary Bloom: 6, 49, 67, 68, 83, 85
    Paulette Braun/Pets by Paulette: 44, 54, 55, 56, 57, 60, 63, 70, 76, 131
    Jeannie Harrison: 59, 65, 69, 74
Production Team: Laura Albert, Beth Brooks, Sean Decker, M. Faunette Johnston,
Carl Pierce, Heather Pope, and Charles Spencer

Contents

First Things First

part one

chapter 1

Dreaming
of
Dogs

Just about every kid wishes for a dog of his or her own—a Lassie to be a faithful companion, or a Rin Tin Tin to play with. Dogs such as these are the stuff of childhood dreams, but dreams don't always reach fulfillment until adulthood. Then, with parental voices echoing—"You can get a dog when you have a place of your own"—the search begins for the ideal dog. Whether you are an adult looking to finally make that childhood dream come true, or a family looking for your child's first pet, somewhere out there is the perfect dog for you—if you know how and where to look.

5

Why Dogs Make Great Pets

People and dogs have been friends since time began. At first, the friendship was cautious, with humans and canines warily taking each other's measure, wily in their desire to make use of each other's talents. People had fire and weapons; dogs possessed speed, keen senses of smell and sight, and sharp teeth for bringing down prey. Together, dog and man were invincible, and they went on to take over the world.

Later, as human society evolved, dogs changed with it. People molded *canis familiaris* to suit a variety of needs. Dogs herded and guarded flocks, kept a watchful eye on property, and developed advanced hunting skills

It's important that you have ample spare time to care for and bond with a dog. (Shetland Sheepdog)

such as flushing and retrieving. Their size ranged from giant to minuscule, depending on their role. Almost anything humans asked, dogs could do, as long as it didn't involve speech or the use of an opposable thumb.

The dog was more than a servant, though. His dark brown eyes peered deep into the soul, inviting secrets. Despite his lack of a voice, he became a trusted confidant and counselor, serving as a sounding board for worries and decisions. When he didn't like someone or something, his hackles rose and his ears flattened, giving silent but eloquent warning of potential danger. Through the ages, the dog has become an integral part of family life, not merely for the contributions he can make as watchdog, hunter or farmhand, but because of his strong love for and desire to be with people. It is that canine enthusiasm—evident in a happy bark and a toothy grin—which draws humans close to dogs and makes them special to us.

Is a Dog for You?

It's easy to see why people get carried away by the desire to own a dog; however, not everyone is suited to dog ownership. It requires a commitment of time and money that can be hard to combine with long working hours, school, sports and other extracurricular activities. Besides the usual requirements of food, water and shelter, dogs need lots of loving interaction. A dog is a social animal that craves contact with his humans. Left alone in a backyard or garage without any playtime, training or petting, he will pine away, or worse, become aggressive in his desire to be with people, leading to problems with jumping and even biting. While the pleasures of a dog's companionship are boundless, so too are the responsibilities. Before you bring home a dog, take a good look at your lifestyle to make sure that a dog's life is really for you.

Before choosing a dog, it's important to determine if a dog is the right kind of pet for your lifestyle. (German Shepherd Dogs)

Evaluate Your Life

The first thing to consider is how often someone is home. Do you and other family members work long or irregular hours, or will it be fairly easy for you to provide a dog with a consistent schedule for meals, walks and playtime? Will you enjoy spending time with a dog when you're at home, or will you be busy paying bills, cooking dinner, and helping the kids with their homework? Even so, it's possible to work in quality time with a dog if you're creative. He'll enjoy watching television with you, lying at your feet while you surf the Internet, or "supervising" homework, woodshop sessions and meal preparation. These are all good opportunities to practice down/stay commands or to make use of a crate or exercise pen so a dog can still be with the family group yet not underfoot.

How Much Space and Time Do You Have?

Where will a dog stay in your home? Will he spend much of his time indoors as part of the family, or are you expecting him to be an outdoor-only pet? The problem with keeping a dog outdoors or in the garage is that he doesn't get the social interaction he needs to

be an emotionally healthy companion. Out of sight, out of mind applies to even the most enthusiastic of dog owners and especially to kids. With proper training and supervision though, even a large dog can fit nicely into a home, so don't automatically consign your new pet to the limbo of outdoor life. He deserves better.

Do you have the time and inclination to train a dog? Puppy kindergarten, starting when he's 10 to 12

It's best to put off dog ownership until your life is calm enough that you are able to handle this large commitment. (Cocker Spaniel)

weeks old, will give you an advantage in housetraining and in general control for grooming and other activities. During puppy kindergarten, potential behavior problems can be nipped in the bud, before a dog becomes too large and unruly to handle. A basic obedience class at 4 to 6 months of age will build on that foundation to teach a dog the good manners he will need to get along in the human world. Regular practice sessions throughout a dog's life are the mortar that will hold your dog-loving house together.

OTHER PETS

Will your other pets adjust well to the presence of a dog? Despite their reputation for being sworn enemies, cats and dogs can actually live together quite peacefully, but it's best to introduce them to each other slowly rather than to simply throw them together and hope for the best. You must also consider the nature of the dog you're interested in getting. Terriers and sighthounds, for instance, love to give chase. It's what they were born for. Will your cat stand her ground and swat them on the nose, or will she turn tail and run? If you choose a breed with a strong prey drive, you'll need to keep close control over any such dog/cat interaction.

A Dog Is For Life

Are you prepared to make a lifetime commitment to a dog? Depending on his breed and level of health, a dog's lifespan can range from a relatively brief 8 years to an unusually lengthy 18 years. You need to consider whether you're at a point in your life that you can make such a long-term commitment. If you're facing a major change, such as college, marriage or divorce, the birth of a child, or frequent business travel, it may

If you're ready for the responsibility, there is a dog out there for you! (Pembroke Welsh Corgi)

be best to put off dog ownership until your life is less hectic. It's not fair to a dog to take him in, develop a relationship with him, and then sell him, give him away, or send him to a shelter because you're unable to give him the attention he needs.

Soul-searching is tough, but in the long run it can save you lots of time, money and heartache. However, if you're ready to share your home and heart with a friend of the canine persuasion, the fun part is about to begin: picking out the perfect dog for you.

chapter 2

Purebred or Mixed Breed?

A dog is a dog is a dog. Or is it? With hundreds of breeds and breed permutations, it's easy to be confused about what type of dog to get. Which is better, purebred or mixed breed? People have been debating that question for years, but the great thing about selecting a dog is that it's a multiple-choice test, and there are no wrong answers. People who want a particular look, coat, temperament, size or working ability generally choose a purebred. Those who want a one-of-a-kind dog or have a desire to save a dog from the pound usually gravitate toward mixed breeds.

Every breed has something special that attracts its followers. Usually a breed's fans cite its personality or temperament, its easy-care coat or long, flowing locks, its rainbow of coat colors or its magnificent white fluffiness. Whether they are talking about Pugs or Pointers, however, they all describe their breeds in much the same way:

Very affectionate toward the family

Great house dog

Very loyal

Loving and protective

Friendly to adults and loves children

Very intelligent and strong

The most remarkable breed ever

Regardless of size, dogs love to be with their people, at work or at play. (Cocker Spaniel)

The above comments are very similar, yet they all describe wildly different breeds. While the genetic diversity of the canine species is astonishing, with its range stretching from the tiny Chihuahua to the towering Irish Wolfhound, all dogs share a unique characteristic: They love people. That quality, combined with the incredible variety of size, appearance and temperament, means that there really is a dog for just about everyone who's willing and able to make the adjustments required to live with one.

Every dog, of whatever kind, has advantages and disadvantages, depending on the needs of the potential owner. What may be an advantage to one person—the beauty of an Afghan Hound's long, lush coat, for instance—may be a disadvantage to another, who doesn't have the time or money to spend on the upkeep such a coat requires. Carefully weighing the

11

pros and cons of a particular dog or type of dog is the first step in making the right choice.

Defining Your Needs

Deciding what kind of dog to acquire is based on a number of considerations, the first of which is whether to get a purebred or a mixed breed. What exactly is a purebred dog? The term purebred means that a dog is descended from parents that belong to a specific breed that has been in existence for many generations, with no other breed being mixed in. (The word thorough-bred is often used interchangeably with purebred, but it more correctly refers to a breed of horse, not a pure-bred dog.) Purebred dogs may have pedigrees—or family trees—that can be traced back for three to five generations and often more.

Many purebred dogs have impressive pedigrees. (Papillon)

While it's true that many breeds were created by mix-ing two or more breeds, once a specific "type" was arrived at and could be reliably reproduced without bringing in other breeds, then that type could be des-ignated as a particular breed. For instance, Doberman Pinschers were created late in the nineteenth century using a mixture of breeds that probably included the German Pinscher, Greyhound, Manchester Terrier and Rottweiler. Once the ideal Doberman was developed, however, breeders only bred Dobermans to Dobermans and no longer used the other breeds to attain a certain look or quality.

Why a Purebred?

People choose purebred dogs for a variety of good reasons. A purebred is generally consistent in size, appearance and temperament. Someone who wants a black, giant-size dog with a long coat, webbed feet and a sweet, caring personality is almost certain to find his or her needs met by a Newfoundland, a working breed with a propensity for water. An apartment dweller who faces limitations on a pet's size can be assured that a toy Poodle will absolutely not grow larger than the 25-pound weight limit. Athletes who run alone or at night may feel more secure in the protective company of a Rottweiler than that of a laid back Greyhound.

Another reason for choosing a purebred might be the desire for a dog with a distinctive appearance. While looks shouldn't be the only reason behind the choice of a dog, they are certainly a factor to consider. There's nothing wrong with preferring a particular color or coat pattern. In as basic a look as white, one can choose from among American Eskimos, Bichon Frisés, Great Pyrenees, Kuvaszok, Maltese, Poodles and Samoyeds. The Dalmatian is renowned for his unique white coat spotted with black or liver. Australian Shepherds, Collies and Corgis often sport fur of a striking bluish gray mixed with splotches of black, a pattern called merle. Some dogs feature striping, which in a distant past may have helped them blend into grasslands or shadows. This striped, or brindle, coat often appears on Greyhounds, Whippets, Bull Terriers, Mastiffs and other breeds.

Purebreds are also valued for their working abilities. Farmers with livestock couldn't do without Australian Cattle Dogs, Border Collies, Great Pyrenees and other herding or flock-guarding breeds. A hunter may select a Chesapeake Bay Retriever for its ability to retrieve in rough conditions, a Labrador Retriever for its all-around capabilities, or a Golden Retriever who will serve double duty as a child's playmate. Golden and Labrador Retrievers, along with German Shepherds, are valued as guide dogs for the blind. And many breeds are noted for their protective natures, which make them ideal family dogs, given the right socialization and training.

Showing or otherwise competing with dogs is a wonderful way to spend time with a pet, make new friends, travel to interesting places and win awards. An interest in competitive events such as conformation showing, obedience trials, field trials and other canine sports can be an incentive to acquire a purebred dog. Purebred dogs with the right qualities and qualifications can earn conformation or field championships, and titles in such performance events as obedience, tracking, earthdog trials, hunt tests, herding, agility, carting, weight-pulling and more. Dog shows and other competitive dog sports are sponsored by the American Kennel Club and the United Kennel Club, by specific breed clubs, or by organizations such as the North American Flyball Association (NAFA) or the United States Dog Agility Association (USDAA). Putting a title on a dog is very satisfying and can be done in a number of arenas.

If you choose a purebred dog, predictions about her future size and demeanor may be more reliable. (Miniature Schnauzer)

DISADVANTAGES OF PUREBREDS

While purebred dogs have many wonderful attributes, they also come with some disadvantages. Among them are price, availability and potential health concerns. Understanding what's behind the cost of a dog, as well as any future costs that may be incurred, are things that will help determine the best choice of pet.

Purebred dogs are expensive. Breeders spend many hours studying pedigrees to determine which dogs will make the best mates for each other and be most likely to produce a fine litter of healthy, well-marked puppies with the proper breed temperament. They spend many dollars at the veterinary clinic, making sure their dogs test clear of venereal diseases and orthopedic, eye, or other hereditary conditions that might be passed on to pups. They bear the expenses of stud fees, shipping the female to the male if he lives in another

Purebreds may be more expensive and less available than mixed breeds. (Standard Poodle)

city or state, ultrasound exams to confirm pregnancies and number of pups, as well as food, veterinary exams and vaccinations for mother and puppies. If the mother has trouble giving birth, a Caesarean section may be required. If she dies or is unable to nurse the puppies, they'll have to be hand-fed around the clock.

Most quality breeders show their dogs until they achieve their conformation championships before breeding them, and some put working titles on their dogs as well. A conformation or working title indicates that other knowledgeable people in the breed believe that the dog is of good quality and suitable for breeding. Showing a dog entails entry fees, travel expenses and sometimes costs for a professional handler.

Supply and Demand

The price of a puppy may also depend on the breed's availability. Depending on your location, the breed you choose, and the quality of the puppy you buy, you can expect to pay anywhere from $300 to $2,500 or more. It may seem that there is an endless supply of Labrador Retrievers, Rottweilers, Dachshunds and Beagles. However, Otterhounds, Cavalier King Charles Spaniels,

Mastiffs and Bloodhounds are less common and may thus command a higher price, even for pet-quality puppies. Expect to pay more for a puppy with show potential. The wait for a rare-breed puppy can be as long as a year or two, or it may entail traveling overseas to find a breeder.

There are fashions in breeds as well. Every time the animated version of Disney's "101 Dalmatians" is released, the popularity of the spotted dogs soars. When a hit movie or television show features a dog of a particular breed, people clamor to own one just like it. The Taco Bell advertising campaign featuring a Chihuahua brought about a tremendous rise in the demand for the diminutive dogs—and a few months later a corresponding rise in the rate of homeless Chihuahuas. Over the years, these same trends have affected Collies, Doberman Pinschers, German Shepherd Dogs, Saint Bernards, Bull Terriers and Jack Russell Terriers.

Fashion affects breed choice, making dogs like Dalmatians popular.

While a popular breed may be easy to find, a good breeder can be more elusive. Surges in a breed's popularity bring out unknowledgeable or unscrupulous breeders who hope their puppies will fetch some of that money people are willing to spend. Like fleas, they feast on a breed's fashionability until they've sucked all the blood out of it, then disappear until the next fad dog comes along. Meanwhile, pet buyers are left with dogs that are ill-suited to their lifestyles or poorly bred pups that may have serious health or temperament problems.

All of these costs are factors in the prices of purebred dogs, yet even so, few responsible breeders make a profit. They breed dogs because they have an interest in working to improve a breed's health, temperament or appearance, or because they value its working ability or its long history. The prices they charge may help them recoup some, but not all, of their costs and are based on the breed's availability in the area and whether the puppy has the right stuff to be a show dog or is simply a nice-quality pet. A good breeder's primary concern is that all the puppies she breeds go to caring homes where they will be loved for a lifetime.

You may find that a mixed breed is more up your alley.

Breed Health

No one wants to have a beloved pet that can't run because she's in pain, or that can't hear the loving words whispered in her ear, or that can't see to chase a ball. So being aware of potential health problems is of major importance in choosing a purebred dog. Genetic diseases of one kind or another are a concern in every breed. Although many breeders work hard to limit or eliminate disease in their dogs, it is not yet a perfect world for purebreds.

Just as with people, some dogs are born with or develop defects or diseases that can cripple or kill them. These include orthopedic conditions such as hip and elbow dysplasia and osteochondritis dissecans; eye problems such as cataracts and progressive retinal atrophy; heart problems such as mitral valve disease and cardiomyopathy; nervous system disorders such as

17

epilepsy; autoimmune problems; and deafness. Although medications and surgery are available to treat many of these conditions, treatment may cost hundreds or even thousands of dollars.

All of these conditions and more are known to be hereditary in nature, and many of them can be tested for before a dog is bred. While good test results can't guarantee that all of a dog's puppies will be healthy, they are an indicator that a breeder has taken steps to help ensure good health.

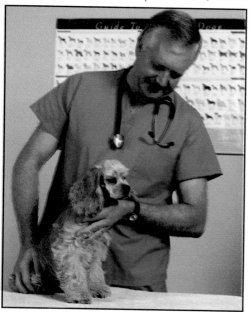

Researching a certain breed's specific health concerns before you make a decision is a good idea. (Cocker Spaniel)

What Is a Mixed Breed?

Maybe a purebred isn't your style. You want something more original, a one-of-a-kind dog. You can't go wrong with the all-American mixed breed. Like snowflakes and fingerprints, no two mixed breeds are alike. They may be the result of a cross between two known breeds, such as a Poodle and a Cocker Spaniel, or they may be of unknown parentage—what's known as a Heinz 57, or a mutt. It's anyone's guess what makes up some of these dogs.

Commonly found mixed breeds are the various Poodle crosses—Cockapoos (Cocker Spaniel and Poodle), Lhasapoos (Lhasa Apso and Poodle) and Schnoodles (Miniature Schnauzer and Poodle)—German Shepherd mixed with Collie or Alaskan Malamute; and Labrador and Golden Retriever crosses. Most often, mixed breeds are born when two dogs get together by accident, but some people breed them deliberately, to see what they'll get, or in an attempt to reproduce a beloved pet.

A Canine Rainbow

There are a lot of good things about mixed-breed dogs. They are just as beautiful, smart and loving as any purebred dog. They come in all shapes, sizes and colors, varied enough to find a place in any home. Some are unique in appearance, one-of-a-kind representatives of the canine species.

Mixed breeds participate just as happily in dog sports as purebreds. Although they can't compete in conformation shows, many performance events are open to them. Mixed breeds perform expertly in obedience, agility, flyball, flying disc competitions and more. They can earn Canine Good Citizen titles from the American Kennel Club and can enter obedience trials sponsored by the American Mixed Breed Obedience Registry. The North American Flyball Association and the United States Dog Agility Association permit mixed breeds in their trials. There are plenty of opportunities for an active dog owner to have a good time with a mixed breed.

Perhaps one of the best things about getting a mixed breed is that the price and availability can't be beat. Animal shelters in every town and city have a large selection of lovable mutts, all just waiting for the right person to come along and make them an offer of a good home. Adoption fees range from free in some cases to $50 or more, which may cover vaccinations, licensing and sometimes spaying or neutering.

Animal shelters offer an endless supply of mixed-breed dogs.

The Luck of the Draw

Like purebreds, mixed breeds have a few drawbacks as well. If they're acquired as puppies, it can be difficult to predict how big they'll grow or what they'll look like as adults. Paw size can sometimes be an indicator, but it's not always very accurate. A puppy that looks like a Lab mix might grow to be the size of a Lab, or she could just keep growing until she looks more like a Newfoundland. For anyone who's not prepared to care for a giant-size dog, that can be quite a shock. Known cross-breeds are more predictable in size, but what the rest of their appearance will be like at maturity isn't always clear.

Mixed-breed puppies are more mysterious all the way around, since you may not be able to determine which breed's genes will be dominant in the adult dog.

Temperament can be a mystery as well. A known mix may take on the personality or temperament attributes of only one parent, or she may be a blend of the two. For instance, a Labrador/German Shepherd mix could be either Ms. Welcome Wagon or Ms. Sharp Edge, depending on whose genes are dominant. But when the background of a pup's parents is unknown, it's hard to know how the personality will develop. Traits such as shyness or aggression can be passed on.

Development of good temperament can also be stunted if a pup leaves her mother and littermates too soon or isn't properly socialized, possibilities that are just as likely with purebreds as with mixed breeds.

It's hard to go wrong with any kind of dog, as long as you take into account your own personality, lifestyle and living environment, things we'll explore in the next chapter.

chapter 3

The **Dog Dating Game**

Deciding what you want in a dog is a lot like choosing a spouse. Issues of compatibility, appearance, sense of humor, grooming and personality are involved in both processes. Size is a factor as well. The best matches take into account the needs of each party when it comes to activity levels, temperament and personality, grooming requirements, trainability, compatibility with children or other pets, amount of living space,  and health concerns. To get started on the search for your canine dream date, make a list of the qualities you want in a dog, using the following questions as a guide.

21

Working Dog or Pet? Protector or Alarm Dog?

What's your purpose for getting a dog? Besides the pure pleasure of companionship, a dog can provide protection or labor, or be a means to an enjoyable hobby, such as conformation showing or the various dog sports. If companionship is your primary goal, go on to the following questions. If you want companionship as well as other qualities, you'll need to think a little further about what you're looking for.

Many people acquire a dog for protection, without considering the level of protection they want. A Chihuahua or Yorkshire Terrier can provide a warning bark just as well as a Doberman Pinscher or a Boxer, and they cost a lot less to feed. Studies have shown that burglars and prowlers are as easily warned off by the bark of a small dog as the bark of a large one. If you feel the need for a higher level of protection, however, consider one of the Working, Terrier or Herding breeds, whose original roles were to play this part for their families.

You may be surprised at the amount of protection a small dog like a Yorkshire Terrier can afford you.

Working dogs are usually found on farms or ranches. They help round up flocks and guard them from predators. On small properties, they may help feed the horses by pulling a cart filled with hay to each stall. Rottweilers are well suited as draft dogs, and many of them retain their original herding and flock-guarding instincts. Border Collies, Australian Shepherds and other herding breeds more than earn their keep doing this kind of work. The talents of the Working and Herding breeds aren't limited to rural homes. Many a smart dog owner has trained her pets to help pick up dirty laundry around the house and pull loads such as yard supplies and groceries.

A 24/7 Friend

How much time will you be able to spend with a dog? In many ways, dogs and humans are very similar, which is probably one of the reasons we get along so well. Both live in packs, or families, and enjoy social inter-action. When we acquire a dog, he adopts us as members of his pack and looks to us for leadership. While full-time employment shouldn't inhibit you from getting a dog, you need to make sure you can balance the time you spend at work with the time a dog needs for care and exercise.

Dogs are creatures of habit, and they'll adapt to whatever schedule you have, as long as they get their share of attention. Some breeds are better than others at entertaining themselves during the day while you're gone. Extremely affectionate breeds, such as Samoyeds or Cavalier King Charles Spaniels, would find a long daily stretch of separation difficult, while a Greyhound, Basset Hound or Scottish Terrier might adapt nicely by sleeping the day away and then

The German Shepherd Dog is an example of a herding dog—whose original instincts are still strong.

spending time with you in the evening. Keep in mind that an easily bored dog, such as a Dachshund, Border Collie or Jack Russell Terrier, may make his own entertainment—of the destructive kind. If you're considering a highly affectionate or "creative" breed, consider getting two so they can keep each other company. And remember that sleeping in your room at night provides a dog with eight hours of bonding time.

23

Size Does Matter

What size dog do you want? Dogs are more diverse than any other species, especially when it comes to size. Chihuahuas, the tiniest members of the dog family, are bred to a standard that calls for them to weigh from two to six pounds, although some go a little larger, up to 12 pounds. They are closely followed by Yorkshire Terriers, which weigh as little as three pounds and should not exceed seven pounds. Depending on whether you judge size by height or weight, Great Danes, Irish Wolfhounds and Mastiffs are the largest dog breeds, with male Danes and Wolfhounds standing 32 inches at the shoulder and male Mastiffs standing a minimum of 30 inches and weighing as much as 230 pounds or more.

Dogs are good at adjusting to your schedule, no matter what it includes! (Border Collie)

Naturally, there are lots of dogs that fall in between those two extremes. You can choose from toy breeds (up to 20 pounds), medium-size dogs (20 to 40 pounds), large dogs (40 to 100 pounds) and giant dogs (more than 100 pounds). While a toy or medium-size dog can fit nicely into just about any size home, large and giant breeds require a little more space, not just in a home or yard but also for transportation. It's a little difficult to squeeze a Mastiff into a Volkswagen Beetle.

That's not to say that you have to rule out a big dog just because you live in a studio apartment. Some giant breeds do very well as city dogs or condominium dwellers, as long as their owners are willing to make the effort to provide them with plenty of wagging space—put those knickknacks above tail level—and daily exercise.

Health care, food and equipment costs vary as well. Because medications are often prescribed according to size, veterinary bills can be higher for a large or giant breed than for one with a little less mass. A jumbo dog can eat four to eight cups of food daily, compared to one-half cup daily for a Chihuahua or a couple of cups for a 15-inch Beagle. A large or giant-size crate or dog-house costs comparatively more than one built for a smaller dog.

Activity Level

How active do I want to be? Some people get dogs as an incentive to exercise. When you have a dog, it's hard to resist those pleading eyes begging for a walk. Other people would just as soon have a dog that will match their stage of couch-potatohood. You can get a dog that will suit any activity level, from flat to flat-out.

If you live in an apartment and crave a large dog, don't lose hope. Some larger dogs do well in cities, as long as they get enough exercise. (Rhodesian Ridgeback)

If you're considering a toy breed, for instance, don't automatically assume that you'll be acquiring a low-energy pet. Toy breeds range from stay-at-home decorator items to miniature go-getters. Even within a breed, there can be quite a difference in a dog's desire for action.

Yorkshire Terriers have a true terrier temperament and are far from being lap dogs. Cavalier King Charles Spaniels and Chihuahuas love a lap as much as any dog, but plenty of them are just as fond of hiking (even up to distances of three or four miles) agility, flyball, tracking and other dog sports.

Grooming

How much time do you have to spend on grooming? Dogs can have short, medium, long, curly or wiry coats. Coat care can be as simple as buffing a Beagle's coat weekly with a hound glove or as complicated as brushing, combing, bathing and drying the long, silky locks of an Afghan Hound or the dense, curly coat of a Standard Poodle.

Grooming has degrees of difficulty. Like the Beagle, the Afghan can get by with weekly grooming; it will just take a lot longer. The same is true of the Pekingese and the Pomeranian. A Poodle in full coat, however, requires daily combing and brushing, as do the Maltese, Lhasa Apso, Shih Tzu and Yorkshire Terrier. A coated breed can be clipped for easier care, but if you chose a particular breed for its appearance—an Old

The Pug is an example of a dog that sheds lightly.

English Sheepdog, for instance—clipping will certainly alter its looks. Some terrier breeds must be hand-stripped of dead hair if their coats are to retain the trademark texture. A clippered terrier coat will feel soft instead of harsh.

If you don't have time for grooming but want to retain your breed's distinctive appearance and ensure that your dog is clean and healthy, you'll need to use the services of a professional groomer. Depending on the amount of work involved, your dog may need to visit the groomer weekly, monthly or quarterly, at a cost per visit of $20 and up.

Shedding is another consideration. All dogs drop dead hair; some just do it more than others. If dog hair on furniture is your worst nightmare, be prepared to follow your pet around with a lint roller. Breeds that shed heavily include German Shepherd Dogs, Australian Shepherds, Bearded Collies, Belgian Tervuren, Sheepdogs and Malinois, Collies, Shetland Sheepdogs, Newfoundlands, Saint Bernards, Alaskan Malamutes,

Akitas, Samoyeds, Norwegian Elkhounds, American Eskimos, Bulldogs, Chow Chows, Keeshonden and Borzoi.

Among the light shedders are most terriers, especially Silky, Yorkshire and Boston Terriers, then Poodles, Pugs, Shih Tzus, Bichon Frises, French Bulldogs and Lhasa Apsos.

Most other breeds fall somewhere in between. Shedding usually occurs seasonally, in the spring and fall, so you can always comfort yourself with the thought that the flurry of hair won't last forever.

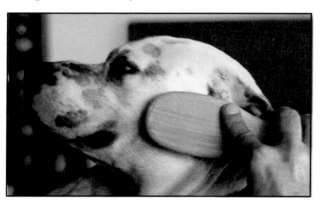

Even dogs with short coats require some grooming. (American Pit Bull Terrier)

Health Concerns

Are you aware of and prepared to deal with health problems in a particular breed? Every breed is prone to some kind of hereditary disease, either because of a small gene pool or because of the close breeding necessary to produce dogs of consistent quality. Inbreeding and linebreeding can be done successfully, but they also increase the risk that problem genes will be reproduced as well. Among the hereditary conditions that can affect purebred dogs are orthopedic problems (bone and joint deformities), heart disease, skin disease and eye disease.

Not every dog will develop these diseases, and diet and environment can also affect whether a problem develops. For instance, puppies that are allowed to get too fat or that are introduced to strenuous exercise such as

27

jumping before they're physically mature (about 18 months old) are more prone to orthopedic problems. When you choose a purebred, determining the health of the breed and finding a breeder who works to prevent hereditary disease will play an important role in making a successful purchase.

ADOPTING A RETIRED SHOW DOG

If you'd like to have an older dog but prefer a purebred, consider acquiring one that didn't make it as a show dog, or is retired from the show ring or from breeding. Breeders often prefer to place these dogs in homes where they'll get individual attention, rather than just being one of the pack or being left behind when it's time to go to the show. This type of adoption is great for the person who wants to know a dog's health and behavioral history or who has an interest in a specific breed. To find a retired dog who is up for adoption, contact breeders just as you would if you were looking for a puppy.

Good with Children

Will a dog be good with children? The age of your children is a major factor in the type of dog you choose. Many breeders, especially of toy breeds, won't sell to families whose children are less than six years old. Very young children don't have the motor skills or emotional capacity to pet a dog gently or refrain from pulling his ears and tail. Toy breeds are at high risk of injury from unintentional mishandling by toddlers. Very young children are also a handful in and of themselves. You may want to wait until your child is at least 3 or 4 years old before you add a dog to the household.

A good canine playmate has a high energy level and a high tolerance for horseplay. He's large enough not to be hurt if a toddler stumbles against him and patient enough to put up with being used as a handhold for a child learning to walk. Golden and Labrador Retrievers fall into this category, as do many of the Working breeds, such as Boxers, Mastiffs and Newfoundlands.

Nonetheless, no matter how loving and protective a dog is, he should not be considered a nanny. Dogs and young children should never be left alone together. There's simply too much room for accidents to occur. The most well-meaning dog can injure or even kill a child by grabbing and shaking her by the neck, just as he might discipline an unruly puppy. And even the most patient of dogs can snap if teased unmercifully. Parental supervision is a must for dog-child interactions.

Older children, eight years and up, are more responsible and can begin to take on the care of a toy breed, for instance, or a dog that requires grooming, such as a Cocker Spaniel or Lhasa Apso. A child this age is also able to attend training classes or participate in 4-H or junior showmanship programs. He can bear some of the responsibility for feeding and exercising the dog, with a sharp parental eye making sure the dog isn't neglected.

Most dogs make ideal companions for children.

Gender Preference

Male or female? Both sexes have advantages and disadvantages. Males are larger but often have the sweetest temperaments. They will mark their territory, though, by lifting a leg on whatever they think needs to be identified as their own. Some people believe females are less distractable, which can be important if you plan to work your dog or participate in sports. They may also be more watchful and more likely to alert you to anything strange going on.

Whichever sex you choose, it's best to spay or neuter a pet. Neutering a male nips mounting behavior and territorial marking problems in the bud and reduces the likelihood of aggression toward people or other dogs. It also precludes the development of testicular tumors or prostate problems. Spaying a female before her first heat greatly reduces her chances of developing mammary tumors and eliminates the possibility of uterine infections or cancer. Spayed or neutered dogs won't get fat unless they don't get enough exercise and are allowed to eat too much. One dog owner's rule: If your dog is fat, you aren't getting enough exercise.

Both male and female dogs have special qualities to offer. (Siberian Huskies)

Age

Puppy or adult? Puppies are loads of fun. Few things in life are more entertaining than watching a puppy roll and tumble, chase his tail, and give a little puppy growl as he pounces on and "kills" his toys. But with puppy fun comes the other puppy f-word: frustration. Puppies have accidents in the house, puppies chew, puppies will get into anything that's not up high or nailed shut. They need constant supervision to keep them out of harm's way. If you get a puppy, you'll need to be meticulous about picking up your clothes and putting breakables out of reach.

Puppies require an extra investment of time as well. They eat three to four meals a day while they're growing, and they need to go out to eliminate frequently. Housetraining is made easier when a puppy is on a regular schedule. Even if you paper-train or litter box-train him, he'll eventually need to learn to go potty outside, unless he's a very small dog that you plan to keep indoors all the time. All of these things are made easier when there's someone home during the day.

For some people, though, the laughter and entertainment a puppy provides is worth more than all the hassle of bringing him up. The bond with a puppy is a special thing, so if you're willing to make the effort, don't hesitate to bring one into your home and heart.

Puppies may require more care than you have time for. Adult dogs often need less training and have passed the frustrating puppyhood stage. (Australian Cattle Dogs)

Nevertheless, older dogs have their advantages. It's a good bet that they are already housetrained, and they may even have some obedience training. They already have their permanent teeth, so they won't be using your prized Chippendale table as a chew toy (unless, of course, they get bored because there is nothing else to chew). They've settled down from puppyhood and are more content to lie by your side or be a lap dog than a rambunctious puppy would be. If you've never owned a puppy—or haven't had one since childhood—you might not realize how much energy they have. Keeping up with a puppy is as tiring as chasing after a toddler and requires just as much patience. All in all, an older dog is less likely to need the close supervision required by a puppy, so he can remain reliably in the house or yard when you're not at home. If you want a peaceful pet, avoid the trials and tribulations of puppyhood and go right for an adult dog.

Taking a chance on a preowned dog, even one with high mileage, brings special rewards. Many people who have adopted mature or even geriatric dogs say their new companions have brought them untold pleasure and seem to be grateful for their second chance at a happy home. If your goal is to save a life, you can't do better than to adopt an adult dog—one year or older—from an animal shelter, humane society or rescue group. If you're willing to exchange the transitory pleasures of puppyhood for the long-term satisfaction of developing a relationship with a dog who needs a second chance, adopting an adult dog will make you happy indeed.

Sometimes adopting an older dog is the best route. If you take home an oldie but a goodie, you will be saving a life as well as gaining a companion. (Sealyham Terrier)

Expenses

How much can you afford to spend on a dog? As discussed previously, costs for food and medication vary according to size. Figure out how much you can afford to set aside for food and veterinary care, and make sure it will be enough to cover the needs of your chosen dog. For example, it will cost about $550 per year to feed three cups a day of a premium dog food. That's about how much a 45- to 50-pound dog would eat. Annual veterinary care for a healthy dog of this size will probably run $200 to $300, including an annual exam, vaccinations, a dental cleaning, heartworm medication, and flea-control products. You'll want to build in a little extra for emergencies such as a serious illness or accident. Don't forget to include expenses for professional grooming if that's something the breed you choose will need.

While purebreds are used as examples in the above questions, you'll want to ask yourself the same things if you're planning to get a mixed breed. When it comes to size, food, activity level, veterinary costs and so on, a dog is a dog is a dog. Read on to find out more about different breed types. The information will guide you in making the right decision, whether your intent is to buy from a breeder or adopt from a shelter or a breed rescue organization.

The
Nitty

part two

Gritty

chapter 4

Profiles by Group

Humans are organizers. We like to have everything labeled and neatly categorized. And we have done so with dogs. The American Kennel Club divides dogs into seven different groups, based on their purpose: Sporting, Hound, Working, Terrier, Toy, Non-Sporting and Herding. Registries such as the United Kennel Club, the Canadian Kennel Club and other foreign kennel clubs make similar divisions.

The following 50 breeds are the most popular of the 140 or so registered by the AKC. They are listed by group, in order of popularity within the group. You'll find a brief overview of each group's general characteristics before the individual breed listings.

The Sporting Group

These dogs have been bred to work closely with people, so they tend to have friendly, willing temperaments. Because their original purpose was to point, flush or retrieve game (and sometimes all three), with the ability to work all day long, these breeds generally have a high energy level. No one has told them that in the new millennium, hunting is primarily a weekend or occasional pastime. They won't be satisfied to live a life of leisure—they're dogs of action and will do best with families who can fulfill their need to run or otherwise be active. Long walks, running, jogging, chasing a ball and sports such as flyball are their favorite activities. The retrievers, for instance, will chase balls all day long if you'll just throw them. The spaniels are probably the most laid back members of this group. Most sporting breeds are easy to train with gentle, positive methods, so they're a good choice for beginning dog owners who can give them an outlet for their energy.

LABRADOR RETRIEVER

His gregarious nature, desire to please and status as a retrieving fool have all made the Labrador America's favorite dog. Throw something, anything, and this dog will bring it back, even if it means splashing through cold water to do it. Originally, the fisherman's friend on the Newfoundland coast, the water-loving dogs made their way to England where sportsmen recognized their talent and developed them into the Lab of today.

The Labrador Retriever is an American favorite.

Males stand 22½ to 24½ inches at the shoulder and weigh 60 to 75 pounds. Females are proportionately smaller. The short, hard coat—in basic black, yellow, or chocolate—repels water and should be brushed about three times a week to keep it glossy and to remove dead hair. Wagging his distinctive otter tail—thick and round at the root, gradually tapering to the tip—the Labrador delights in playing with kids, going hunting, bringing home ribbons from obedience and field trials, or doing anything else his owners can think of to teach him, especially if it involves water. Thanks to his trainability, he also excels as a guide and service dog, and is the most widely used breed for those jobs.

This is a large, high-energy dog that needs lots of activity to be happy. For the most part, he's a healthy breed, but be aware of potential problems, including hip dysplasia, epilepsy and progressive retinal atrophy. Buying from a caring, reputable breeder is your best safeguard against health problems.

GOLDEN RETRIEVER

Versatile, intelligent and charming, Golden Retrievers make wonderful guide dogs and get along well with children.

Graced with a sunny personality and quintessential canine good looks, the Golden Retriever makes friends with everyone he meets. This sporting dog was developed in mid-19th century England, probably from a mixture that included a yellow retriever, the Tweed Water Spaniel, and the Bloodhound.

The breed's soft mouth and trainability make him prized by hunters, but he's also a beloved family pet who can be a child's best playmate. Responsive and quick to learn, the Golden brings home high scores at obedience trials and willingly learns tricks, games or anything else you can teach. This intelligence and versatility make him a favorite among guide dog trainers as well.

Goldens are large, with males standing 23 to 24 inches at the shoulder and weighing 65 to 75 pounds; females are proportionately smaller. The Golden is adorned with a wavy or straight coat that's dense and water-repellent. The color, for which the dog is named, ranges from the bright gold of a guinea coin to the pale gold of champagne. A good brushing about three times a week will keep the coat gleaming.

This breed loves people and will enjoy life to the fullest with an active, loving family. Among the hereditary problems that can affect the breed are hip dysplasia and cataracts, so choose your breeder carefully.

COCKER SPANIEL

The merry Cocker is the smallest member of the Sporting Group. While it was once identical to the English Cocker, fifty years of American breeding led to the development of a different type, and the breed eventually split, with the American Cocker going on to become one of the most well-loved breeds in this country, a status he still retains today.

At the height of his popularity, the Cocker's sweet temperament was almost destroyed through overbreeding, but responsible breeders are working hard to restore the breed's reputation as a smart, loving, friendly pet.

The American Cocker Spaniel is in a class all his own.

Cockers come in three color varieties: black, particolor (white with markings in another color), or any solid color other than black. The luxuriant coat sheds, but not heavily. It does, however, require a thorough daily brushing to keep mats from forming. The breed can be prone to skin and ear problems, so if you choose a Cocker, keep on top of this breed's grooming needs. The Cocker has a moderate activity level and is a medium-size dog that stands 14½ to 15½ inches at the shoulder, so it's well suited to just about any size home in city or country.

A few members of the breed still retain their gundog abilities and have proven themselves in the field, but most are happy to spend their lives as family pets who love nothing more than playing with the kids or curling up on the sofa with their people. Potential health problems to be aware of are hip dysplasia, luxating patellas and epilepsy.

GERMAN SHORTHAIRED POINTER

The 17th-century German sportsman wanted a handsome, all-purpose gundog that could hunt fur or feather, on land or in water. The German Shorthaired Pointer is what he came up with. Known as the Kurzhaar in Germany, this breed is skilled at tracking, pointing and retrieving game. To top it all off, he's a good watchdog and companion.

The German Shorthaired is a high-energy family sportsman and companion.

The German Shorthair was brought to North America in the 1920s, and he's now popular in the field and in the home. Not surprisingly, he's highly energetic and needs plenty of daily exercise to prevent him from turning destructive out of boredom. He likes being part of the family and will be unhappy if left out in the yard all the time. His size makes him best suited to a suburban or country home.

Males stand 23 to 25 inches at the shoulder and weigh from 55 to 70 pounds; females are 2 inches shorter and 10 pounds less. The German Shorthair sports a hard, dense, short coat that may be solid liver in color or liver and white with ticking, liver patched and white ticked, or liver roan. The coat doesn't shed much and is easily kept in shape with a weekly brushing. The German Shorthair is amenable to training, but begin early if you plan to use him in the field.

ENGLISH SPRINGER SPANIEL

As bouncy as his name, the Springer is a high-energy dog that enjoys life to the fullest. Eager to please and quick to learn, this largest of the land spaniels—which takes its name from its job of "springing" game for the hunter's net—makes a fine family friend, hunting companion and watchdog.

The Springer Spaniel stands 17 to 21 inches at the shoulder, with females being on the smaller side. A flat or wavy coat comes in liver or black and white; tricolor; or roan in blue or liver. The coat sheds water, dirt and debris picked up outdoors, but the dog still needs a good brushing several times a week to remove dead hair and keep it looking nice. A little trimming on the head, throat and around the feet gives the dog a neat appearance. Don't forget to check and clean the ears frequently. They pick up foxtails and other foreign bodies and are prone to long-lasting infections if they get too dirty. Daily exercise, kind, consistent training, and being part of the family will keep this dog effervescent.

BRITTANY

Agile and quick to learn, this breed was created in the mid-19th-century to be a versatile gundog in the French province of Brittany. Its forebears probably included the English Setter, Welsh Springer Spaniel and several small French land spaniels. The Brittany's fame as a dog that could point, retrieve, and work well in dense cover or open country ensured the breed's spread to England and the United States. Unlike other spaniel breeds, the Brittany's orange and white or liver and white coat is only lightly fringed, so it's easy to keep tangle-free with weekly brushing.

Their size makes Brittanys suited to any home from a condo to a castle; they stand $17\frac{1}{2}$ to $20\frac{1}{2}$ inches at the shoulder and weigh 35 to 45 pounds. These dogs are born to the sporting life but they aren't as fervent about it as a Labrador or Chesapeake Bay Retriever might be. Brittanys are happy to take a couple of daily walks with the family during the week and go hunting on the weekend. They're smart, but training sometimes requires a firm hand. Harshness, however, is counterproductive. In general, this is a healthy breed, although skin problems occur occasionally.

Born to the sporting life, Brittanys are most content when playing outside with their people.

WEIMARANER

This sporty German import bears the nickname Gray Ghost, not only for his striking steel-gray color but also for his endearing habit of dogging his owner's footsteps. Developed at the court of the Grand Duke Karl August of Weimar, the Weimaraner was originally used to hunt deer, bear and boar. Over the years, though, the numbers of big game decreased, and the dog's excellent nose was put to work on birds instead. He was found to be a superb all-purpose gundog, and German sportsmen valued him highly, taking steps to control breeding so that the Weimaraner's qualities would remain intact. Eventually, an American joined their tight little circle and was permitted to bring two Weimaraners to the United States.

Today's Weimaraner is still a fine hunting dog, used almost entirely on small fur and feathered game, but he's an excellent family dog as well, loyal and protective. His high energy level makes him a good companion for kids. He learns quickly and is a good competitor in obedience and agility. Best suited to suburban or country life, the Weimaraner needs an hour or two of daily exercise.

Aristocratic in appearance, this is a large breed, with males standing 25 to 27 inches at the shoulder, females 2 inches shorter. The Weimaraner is a fairly healthy breed, but be sure to buy from a breeder who x-rays breeding stock for hip dysplasia. The short, sleek coat comes in shades of mouse-gray to silver-gray, with harmonizing eyes, nose and lip pigmentation. A good weekly brushing burnishes the coat to its shining best.

Weimaraner fans adore the gorgeous gray coats for which the breed is known.

VIZSLA

Once known as the Hungarian Pointer, the Vizsla is probably a relatively modern breed, developed in Hungary sometime before the start of World War I in 1914. It is a versatile pointing breed, well respected for its abilities as gundogs. The horrors of two world wars almost brought about the breed's demise, but

Hungarian breeders made a concerted effort to save it, and it is now known as the national dog of Hungary.

American sportsmen began importing the Vizsla in the 1950s, and he's now well known as an all-around hunting dog with an excellent nose. A strong swimmer that is easily trained, the Vizsla works equally well on waterfowl and upland game. He's a large breed but lightly built, with males standing an average of 23 inches at the shoulder, females 22 inches. Weight ranges from 50 to 65 pounds for males, 40 to 55 pounds for females.

Because he's a sporting breed, the Vizsla has a high activity level and needs plenty of daily outdoor exercise, but given that, he can be comfortable in a large apartment or small house. His short, dense coat is a golden-rust color that's kept gleaming with a weekly

The Vizsla is an easily trained sporting dog who needs a lot of exercise.

brushing. The Vizsla is an excellent watchdog and a good companion for children. Look for a puppy that comes from bloodlines that are free from epilepsy, and ask if the breeder x-rays breeding stock for hip dysplasia.

The Hound Group

Hounds can be divided into two types: sighthounds and scenthounds. The sighthounds are the Ferrari of the dog world, sleek and speedy, while the scenthounds are more akin to a Honda Accord, well built and utterly reliable in their work. Each has its charms. All the hounds are alike, however, in their independent natures. Tracking game often required them to work away from their handlers, so they had to learn to think for themselves. If you want a dog that will obey your every command without hesitation, a hound is not for you. Hounds also require a secure yard and walks on a leash, because their instincts to chase or to follow intriguing movement or scents are overwhelming. A sighthound that's not restrained by a leash will take off in an instant after a moving object such as a cat, rabbit or even a galloping horse. A scenthound might not move so quickly, but he'll wander right away from home in pursuit of an unusual odor. These dogs love food, and the term chowhound applies especially to them. They'll gobble down whatever's in reach, and some of them are just the right height to snack off the dinner table or kitchen counter. In the right home, these dogs can be perfect matches. Sighthounds will most likely prefer homes with older children, while scenthounds generally have the patience and stamina to deal with younger kids.

DACHSHUND

With two sizes and three coat types, there's a Dachshund for everyone who's intrigued by this comical dog with the short legs and long back. The breed's ancestors were used in Europe to hunt badger, fox and sometimes even larger game, and the breed today retains a tenacious, alert personality. This is a mischievous breed that's friendly and curious, although poorly bred specimens are known to be aggressive toward people or other animals. His loud and repetitive bark makes the Dachshund a great (albeit sometimes annoying) watchdog.

This Dachshund is representative of the longhaired variety, one of the three types of coats a Dachshund may have.

Dachshunds come in miniature and standard sizes, with the minis being 11 pounds and under, the standards 16 to 32 pounds. Both fit well into any size household. They may have smooth, long or wirehaired coats that come in a variety of colors such as solid red, black and tan, chocolate, gray, dapple or brindle. Each variety has its own personality, with the longhairs being laid back, the wirehairs clownish, and the smooths falling somewhere in the middle of those extremes.

Naturally, the longhaired Dachshund requires the most frequent grooming, about three times a week, but a weekly brushing will take care of the wirehair and the smooth. To prevent infection, keep the long, hanging ears clean and dry. The Dachshund's long backs make some prone to disc problems, especially if they're allowed to get fat, so don't let these chowhounds overeat. Limit treats to training sessions; these dogs are highly motivated by food, and it's a good way to get them to pay attention. Dachshunds do best in homes with older children who won't treat them roughly. In good condition, they're capable of going on long walks and participating in dog sports such as agility, but when the weather's bad or time is short, they can get by with a play session in the yard or even indoors.

The popular Beagle has been a favorite family pet for decades.

BEAGLE

Whether he's trailing a rabbit, sniffing his way around the show ring, or simply being a loveable family pet, the Beagle retains the cheerful yet workmanlike character that has made him popular for many decades. The breed was originally developed to accompany hunters on foot, who might spend all day hunting a single hare. This called for a dog with a good nose, persistence and stamina, but not necessarily speed.

Packs of Beagles were kept by lesser landed gentry and well-to-do farmers who might not have the resources to keep packs of the larger Foxhounds, which the Beagle resembles in miniature.

The Beagle's two favorite activities are eating and following scents, and his activity level and love of fun make him a good companion for kids. As a bonus, he's a good watchdog, barking to alert the household whenever anyone approaches. He comes in two sizes: 13 inches and under, and over 13 inches, but not over

15 inches. Either size is a comfortable fit for most households. This breed is prone to obesity, so don't let him overeat. The Beagle is dapper in a short, hard, easy-care coat that may be any acceptable hound color or combination of colors. A weekly going-over with a hound glove and regular ear cleaning and nail trimming will meet his grooming needs. This is an active dog that needs plenty of daily outdoor exercise. A securely fenced yard is a must to keep the Beagle from following his nose away from home and into trouble.

Basset Hound

With his mournful expression, short legs, and long, sweeping ears, the Basset Hound stands out from the pack. While he may look like a couch potato at first glance, an interesting scent will soon lure him onto the trail of a rabbit or other small game, and he'll keep going and going and going. It's no wonder he has long been the symbol for Hushpuppy shoes.

The Basset Hound's popularity can be attributed to his love of children, sense of humor, prowess as a watchdog and ease of care.

The Basset Hound originated in France, where packs of the dogs were used to trail game. The breed takes its name from the French word *basset*, meaning low-set, a physical advantage that made him well suited for moving through dense cover. This sturdy hound is still worked in packs today in a slow-moving rabbit hunt called basseting, but most often he's found as a family pet who's equally at home in town or country. His popularity can be attributed to his love of children, sense of humor, prowess as a watchdog and ease of care.

The Basset's short coat comes in black, tan and white, or a combination of the three. A weekly brushing with a hound glove removes dead hair and keeps the coat glossy. This breed's ears and eyes are prone to infection, so they should be inspected regularly for dirt, discharge or foreign bodies. The Basset will enjoy a daily walk, but when he's at home, make sure the yard is secure or he may go wandering off in search of whatever smells good.

The Working Group

Serious is the watchword for these brainy, brawny dogs, talented in many different ways. Bred to guard property and people, catch poachers, guard flocks from predators, or to haul goods in carts, wagons or sleds, they are large, strong and smart.

If you want more than a dog that barks in warning, a member of the working group is a good choice, but be prepared to give him plenty of early training and socialization. Because of their power and assertive natures, working breeds can be dangerous in the hands of an inexperienced owner who doesn't give them the respect they deserve. They respond best to firm but fair training and will respect you in turn.

Because large breeds are prone to hip and elbow dysplasia, choose your breeder carefully, and make sure your puppy doesn't put on weight too quickly or engage in activities such as jumping until he's physically mature, at about 18 months of age. Activities these breeds will enjoy and excel at include hiking, jogging, carting, weight pulling and obedience trials, to name just a few. The working breeds are protective of home and family and will guard children with their lives, but they aren't meant to be babysitters except under parental supervision.

ROTTWEILER

This powerful dog takes his name from the German market town of Rottweil, where he was known as the butcher's dog. His job was to drive cattle to market and guard the proceeds on the way home, a task for which he was ideally suited, given his strength and protective nature. When railroads and motorized vehicles came

along, the Rottweiler was put out of work and almost disappeared, but German doglovers took an interest in the breed and worked to save it. Today, he's one of the most popular dogs in the United States, thanks to his reputation for fearlessness and devotion. Because he's so strong and smart, though, he's not right for every home.

The Rottweiler has a mind of his own, and he needs an owner who can match him in intelligence and will. Consistent, firm (not harsh) training, early socialization and lots of exercise are necessary to keep him from running the household. Rottweilers stand 22 to 27 inches at the shoulder, with females being on the smaller side. Their short, harsh coats are black with rich tan markings. Weekly brushing, nail trimming, and eye and ear care will keep the Rottie in top condition. This breed loves children and will tolerate a lot from them, but supervision is a must, especially when neighboring children are visiting. The Rottweiler will step in to set things right if he thinks "his" child is being mistreated by a playmate. Hip dysplasia and temperament are concerns in this breed, so be sure and choose your breeder carefully.

Rottweilers are one of the most popular dogs in the United States thanks to their reputation for fearlessness and devotion.

BOXER

The Boxer is a product of fine German engineering, a blend of a mastiff-type dog and a Bulldog that resulted in a medium-size protection dog with a short, easy-care coat. Created in Germany a little more than a century ago, the agile Boxer, named for his defensive habit of

punching with his paws, was first registered with the AKC in 1904. He stands up to 25 inches at the shoulder and has a chiseled head that gives him a look of nobility. Ears may be cropped or natural, but the tail is usually docked.

The Boxer's sleek coat comes in shades of fawn or brindle with white markings. A weekly going over with a hound glove or bristle brush keeps the coat shiny and helps reduce the moderate level of shedding. Boxers are family dogs through and through, adapting well to any size household. They love kids and are

The Boxer is a low-maintenance, family-friendly dog.

excellent protectors of the home. They're highly energetic, however, and need lots of exercise to keep them occupied and out of trouble.

SIBERIAN HUSKY

This dog is a descendant of dogs bred by the Chukchi people, who made their home in the harsh environment of the Siberian Arctic. To pull their sleds, loaded with game, the Chukchi needed dogs that were small and quick, able to travel great distances and work for long periods without much food. When they weren't pulling sleds, the Chukchi dogs turned their talents toward herding reindeer. At night, they cozied up with the family to provide much-needed warmth, so their status as house dogs goes back a long way. Siberians gained fame in the winter of 1925, when a team driven by Gunnar Kassen helped deliver diphtheria serum to disease-ravaged Nome, Alaska. Their race against death is commemorated by a statue of the lead dog, Balto, which stands in Central Park, New York.

Today's Siberian is an athletic dog that enjoys the outdoors. He's a great companion for anyone who enjoys such sports as hiking, biking, skating and jogging. This is a highly active dog that needs a family who can keep up with him. He loves kids and gets along well with other dogs. At rest, the Siberian's foxy tail trails behind him, but when he's on the alert it's carried over his back. They come in all colors, including white. The breed's off-standing double coat is thick and soft and of medium-long length. Brush the coat one to three times a week to remove dead hair and distribute skin oils.

The Siberian Husky is a highly active, loving dog.

Like other spitz type breeds, the Siberian sheds heavily in warm weather. They are medium-size dogs that stand 20 to 23½ inches at the shoulder and weigh 35 to 60 pounds, with females on the smaller side. The Siberian can adapt to city life, as long as he gets plenty of exercise; but at heart, he's a dog who loves the great outdoors. He's people-oriented, so his watchdog abilities aren't the greatest. Like the Chukchi people who created him, the Siberian is a nomad, so keep him from roaming with a leash and a securely fenced yard. Buy from a breeder who tests breeding stock for hip dysplasia and eye disorders.

DOBERMAN PINSCHER

Tax collector Louis Dobermann created this breed to accompany him on his rounds and protect him from irate taxpayers. Among the breeds he probably used to develop the sleek, elegant Doberman Pinscher were the Greyhound, the German Pinscher, the Manchester

51

Terrier and the Rottweiler. From them, the new breed took grace, speed, tenacity, protectiveness and its distinctive coloration. Although he's famed as a security dog, the Doberman is also a loving family companion

Although famed as a security dog, the Doberman is also a loving family companion that's fond of children and excels in obedience trails.

that's fond of children and excels in obedience trials. Firm, early and consistent training will keep the Doberman from running the household.

This is a large breed, with males standing 27½ inches at the shoulder, females slightly less. The short, shiny coat comes in black, red, blue or fawn, all with rust markings above each eye, on the muzzle, throat and forechest, legs and feet, and beneath the tail. Weekly brushing and regular nail, ear and dental care are all the grooming needed. The ears are usually cropped to a point, but there's nothing wrong with leaving them natural. The Doberman adapts well to life in the city or country, but he needs daily exercise to maintain his trim figure. Health problems to be aware of are cardiomyopathy, a heart disorder, and wobblers syndrome, which affects the spinal column.

GREAT DANE

Known as the Apollo of Dogs for his handsome looks and noble demeanor, the Great Dane is a giant among dogs, not just in size but also in heart. Sixteenth-century European noblemen hunted wild boar with the huge dogs, which were probably a mixture of hound and mastiff. The dogs also guarded estates and were fearsome combatants in battle. The brave but friendly Great Dane we know today was developed in 19th-century Germany. He makes a wonderful family companion and watchdog, but parents of young children should note that this breed can knock a toddler down with a swipe of his tail. That warning applies as well to people with lots of breakables; that wagging tail can clear a coffee table in seconds!

Great Danes stand 28 to 32 inches or more at the shoulder, so their looks alone are more than enough to give a burglar the shakes, especially when combined with their deep, threatening bark. Like many large and giant breeds, the Great Dane is prone to hip dysplasia and other orthopedic problems, so it's important that he not put on weight too quickly as a puppy. Gastric torsion is also a concern in this breed, so most breeders recommend restricting his exercise and water intake immediately after meals. Weekly brushing is enough to maintain the short, smooth coat, which comes in brindle, fawn, blue,

The Great Dane is known as the "Apollo of Dogs."

black or harlequin (white with black patches). Ears may be left natural or cropped to a point. With daily exercise and a little room to stretch out, the Great Dane can be happy in either a rural or urban setting.

SAINT BERNARD

The usual cliché is that a particular breed is a big dog in a small package. Not so with the Saint Bernard, which has been described as a small dog in a big package. This gentle, noble giant loves attention, yet doesn't demand it. Instead, he's there to please his people, being willing to do just about anything that's asked of him.

While the Saint Bernard as we know it today didn't really begin to take form until the mid-19th-century, dogs of that type have been known in Swiss valleys since before the Romans came, making a place for themselves on Swiss farms and estates, serving as watchdogs, guardians and draft animals.

The Saint is a giant breed, standing a minimum of $27\frac{1}{2}$ inches at the shoulder (males); females measure 2 inches shorter. His short or medium-length coat can be red with white or white with red. The chest, feet, tail tip, head and neck should have white markings. The coat sheds heavily and should be brushed thoroughly about three times a week. Check the eyes for discharge and clean them as needed. Place hand towels strategically around the house; you'll need them to wipe up the drool.

This Saint Bernard loves nothing more than to please his people.

This breed needs room to sprawl and will enjoy plenty of daily exercise. Begin training early, before the Saint is too big to control. He loves kids, but his size is enough to bowl over an unsteady toddler. Older children will find him a loving, protective playmate. Giant breeds are prone to serious orthopedic problems if they put on too much weight as puppies, so watch your Saint's weight carefully.

MASTIFF

Except for his great size, it's hard to imagine that the gentle mastiff was once a fierce war dog and a favorite in blood sport competitions, being pitted against lions, elephants and bears. Sometimes called the Old English Mastiff, this breed is now more at home in a family with children to protect and play with. The ferocious nature of yore shows itself only when danger threatens and the dog must place his massive size between his loved ones and harm.

Depending on gender, the mastiff stands $27\frac{1}{2}$ to 30 inches or more at the shoulder, and some weigh more than 200 pounds. The short, dense coat—in shades of apricot, silver fawn or dark fawn-brindle with a darker muzzle, ears and nose forming a mask on the face—is easy to care for with a weekly brushing. This breed drools heavily, so arm yourself with strategically placed hand towels around the house and on your person.

A large home with a yard gives the Mastiff plenty of room to sprawl, but he can adapt to smaller quarters. A one- or two-mile daily walk will meet his exercise needs. As with most giant breeds, orthopedic problems can develop in puppies that put on too much weight too quickly. Other health problems that can affect the Mastiff are cardiomyopathy and eye diseases such as progressive retinal atrophy, cataracts and retinal dysplasia.

BULLMASTIFF

The noble Bullmastiff is descended from both the Roman Mastiff and the English Bulldog. The Bullmastiff's history can be traced back to late 19th century England, but the breed may be considerably older than this. Gamekeepers bred the Bullmastiff to provide quick, agile protection against poachers.

The Mastiff is a noble, ancient breed. She requires plenty of exercise and attention—in return for this, she will be an affectionate, loyal companion.

While slighter in build than the Mastiff, the Bullmastiff is nonetheless a dog of considerable size, with males reaching an average of 25 to 27 inches at the shoulder, and weighing approximately 110 pounds. Females stand about 24 to 26 inches, and weigh from 80 to 90 pounds.

Bullmastiffs thrive in a caring atmosphere where they can find early, reliable training and socialization. Such socialization is a must, given the size (and weight) that your dog will ultimately reach. Though he easily adjusts to an apartment or city dwelling, the Bullmastiff will be most comfortable in a large house where he can do what he does best—settle in and focus on his people. The Bullmastiff is a very sociable dog, and is more ideally suited to the job of being a body-guard than merely a property protector.

Because the Bullmastiff is a large breed, make sure you buy your puppy from a breeder who has breeding stock

x-rayed for hip and elbow dysplasia. Brushing his coat once or twice a week should remove dead hair and keep your dog looking neat and trim. The Bullmastiff does drool, so make sure to keep paper towels througout your home for quick wipe-ups. The Bullmastiff is a calm, dependable dog of great intelligence. Given the appropriate surroundings, your Bullmastiff is sure to become a reliable, gracious companion.

The Bullmastiff is a gentle giant. With proper care, he will make a wonderful companion.

Alaskan Malamute

Hailing from the Great White North, this breed is one of the largest and most powerful members of the spitz family and bears the trademark prick ears and waving plume of a tail. The Alaskan Malamute takes his name from an Inuit tribe, the Mahlemut, who used him to track large game and pull sleds with heavy loads. When he wasn't working, he could often be found snuggled in a cozy pile with the kids. Without the Malamute, Polar expeditions wouldn't have been successful, and the breed served with honor in both world wars.

Today, the Malamute is found in warm climates as well as cold, but he still likes nothing better than burrowing into a snowdrift and taking a nap. This breed requires lots of daily exercise and will especially enjoy accompanying you on cross-country skiing outings. He can even pull you on skis or a sled. Inhabitants of warmer climes will find the Malamute an excellent companion for jaunts on bicycles or inline skates. (Just don't work him too hard in mid-day heat.) This type of regular activity, combined with firm, consistent training, will help keep the Malamute happy and out of trouble.

The Alaskan Malamute is a large dog, standing 23 to 25 inches at the shoulder and weighing 75 to 85 pounds. Because he's a large breed, make sure you buy your puppy from a breeder who has breeding stock x-rayed for hip and elbow dysplasia. Be prepared for the heavy, coarse coat to shed heavily. Brushing about three times a week will help keep the hair under control.

A distinguishing feature of the Alaskan Malamute is his face markings, which consist of a cap over the head with the face being either all white or marked with a bar or mask. The coat comes in a variety of colors and may be solid white, light gray, black, sable, or shadings of sable to red. Affectionate and friendly, the Malamute prefers the great wide open to the confines of city life.

The athletic Malamute prefers wide-open spaces and plenty of exercise.

The Terrier Group

These are the rapscallions of the dog world. Terriers have minds of their own, and they go after what they want. Once known as "earth dogges" for their habit of going to ground after earth-dwelling critters such as moles, foxes and rats. They still love to dig and will excavate your yard if given half a chance. Terriers are also capable of digging out of the yard, so you need to take extra precautions to make sure fences and gates are secure. Some terrier owners are driven to placing trenches lined with concrete or other material beneath their fences. Terriers are smart, high-energy dogs, and you'll need to think a couple of steps ahead of them if you want to remain in charge. They don't respond well to rote training and do best with food rewards and frequent changes of action.

The terrier is definitely a dog who likes to put his own spin on anything he does, so a tolerance for surprises is of value to the person who takes on one of these bright dogs. Terriers can be aggressive toward cats and other dogs, so they need to be under tight control whenever such interactions occur. They're territorial and bark loudly to announce the approach of friend or foe. Terriers can be trained for obedience trials, although they aren't usually among the high scorers, but they excel at games such as agility and, of course, earth dog trials.

MINIATURE SCHNAUZER

Bouncy and loud, the Miniature Schnauzer is a smart, bold, devoted dog who's well loved for his charming, cheerful nature and superb watchdog abilities. He's

the only terrier breed created outside of Great Britain and is the most popular of the bunch. Probably developed by crossing small Standard Schnauzers with Affenpinschers or Poodles, this is a dog that learns quickly and excels in obedience trials.

The Miniature Schnauzer stands up to 14 inches at the shoulder and weighs 14 pounds, more or less, making him just the right size for any home. His solid black,

The Miniature Schnauzer is the most popular of the terrier group.

black and silver, or salt and pepper coat doesn't shed much and can be kept looking nice with about three grooming sessions a week to keep the beard and leg furnishings neat and tangle-free. The services of a professional groomer may be necessary to maintain his distinctive Schnauzer look. The Miniature Schnauzer loves kids, and his high energy level matches their own. Hereditary eye disease is occasionally a problem in this breed.

WEST HIGHLAND WHITE TERRIER

Scottish daring, determination and devotion are all combined in the small white body of the Westie. Kissing cousin to the Cairn Terrier, it was one of the breeds collectively called the Terriers of Scotland, whose purpose was to dig among the rocks and in the dirt in search of their prey: the fox and badger. The Westie's white coloration made him easy to see so his

handler could keep track of him. The breed was developed to its modern form by Col. E. Malcolm of Poltalloch, who was understandably upset when he accidentally shot his favorite brown terrier, thinking it was a hare.

A cunning intelligence combined with friendly self-assurance marks this compact dog, who stands up to 11 inches at the shoulder. He's well suited to city or suburbia and enjoys being with his family, whether on a walk or going for a ride in the car. He

The Westie is well suited to city or suburbia and enjoys being with her family, whether on a walk or going for a ride in the car.

needs daily exercise and may find an outlet in digging if he's not sufficiently entertained. Among the heritable health problems that can affect the Westie are patellar luxation, hernias, Legg-Perthes disease and craniomandibular osteopathy, a temporary but painful jawbone inflammation that can occur in puppies. The breed is also prone to flea allergy dermatitis. For these reasons, choose your breeder carefully. Because his coat is white, the Westie needs a little extra care to keep him looking presentable. Brush and comb him at least three times a week to keep his coat at its best. The hard, wiry coat must be plucked or stripped to retain its texture; using clippers will turn it soft. Professional grooming may be necessary if you want him to have the trademark frame of hair around the face and correct body outline. The Westie is a good watchdog and enjoys the company of kids.

SCOTTISH TERRIER

"Never say die" is the Scottie's motto, and indeed his nickname is the Diehard. Originating as a working terrier in the Scottish highlands, the Scottie started out as just one of several types of terriers known collectively as Scotch Terriers. However, by 1881, enthusiasts had developed a dog called the hard-haired Scotch Terrier, but within a couple of years he became known as the Scottish Terrier, the name he retains to this day. The Scottie is a scrapper toward other dogs, and he takes his time before becoming friendly with people. Toward his family, though, he can be loving, loyal and playful. A fiery, "tails up" attitude and determined nature make him a good watchdog who barks ferociously whenever his territory is approached, even by passers-by across the street. He's not a typical children's pet, given his dignified personality; but if treated with respect, he can certainly get along with them.

The Scottie is loving, loyal and playful toward his family. If treated with respect, he makes a fine children's pet.

Like most terriers, the Scottie can be stubborn, so begin training and socialization early. For the most part the Scottie is a healthy breed, although some are subject to a condition called Scottie cramp, which resembles a brief, slight seizure. Make sure the breeder from whom you buy has bred from dogs that don't have this problem. Most people picture Scotties as classic black, but their hard, wiry coats can also be gray, brindle or wheaten.

Considerable grooming is required to maintain the Scottie's distinctive appearance, and he needs a good brushing about three times a week. The coat can be clipped for ease of care, but as with most wiry coats, this will soften the traditional hard texture. The Scottie is sturdy and low-slung, measuring about 10 inches at the shoulder and weighing 18 to 22 pounds. Whether he lives in an apartment or a house, he'll enjoy a brisk daily walk.

CAIRN TERRIER

Named for the rock piles over which packs of them clambered in search of their prey, Cairn Terriers are native to the Western Highlands of Scotland. True to their earth-dog heritage, they like to dig, especially if they're not kept busy with less destructive activities.

Cairn Terriers may be especially prone to destructive digging if you don't keep them occupied.

Nonetheless, they make fine companions for families with children old enough to treat them with respect. Standing about 10 inches at the shoulder, they are compact bundles of fur with shaggy eyebrows and foxy expressions. Their hard, profuse coats come in all colors except white. Shedding is minimal and can be controlled with weekly combing. The inquisitive Cairn is a good watchdog and has a moderate activity level that will be satisfied with a couple of short daily walks. Among the health problems that you

should be aware of are patellar luxation, Legg-Perthes disease and craniomandibular osteopathy.

61

The Toy Group

Most dogs were developed for a specific purpose, and the toy breeds are no exception. They hold perhaps the most important job of all—that of being a companion. When people were no longer living hand to mouth and had created arts and government, they began to crave some luxuries—among them, small dogs who served no purpose other than adorning the household and adoring their people (along with warming their beds and serving as flea decoys). Toy breeds were known in early Chinese civilizations and in the Roman Empire. In fact, some cynologists (people who study dogs) suggest that the Roman signs "Cave canem"—beware of the dog—actually served to remind people not to step on the little Italian Greyhounds. Their interpretation may be tongue in cheek, but undoubtedly the people of 2,000 years ago loved their tiny dogs just as much as do the pet owners of today.

Although some of them look like stuffed animals, toy breeds are just as much dog as their larger brethren. They have the same instincts and behaviors, they just inhabit a smaller body. Toy dogs are fully capable of being trained; indeed, they need it just as much as any other dog or they're likely to become little Napoleons, running the household with an iron paw, and not necessarily one in a velvet bootie. Nor are they sure to be couch potatoes. There are some toy breeds that will be happy to loll around with you eating bonbons, but many of them have earned titles in obedience, agility, tracking, flyball and other dog sports. Don't underestimate what these dogs are capable of doing. Choose a toy breed if you have plenty of time to spend with it. These dogs were bred to be companions, and they'll be unhappy if they sit at home alone all day. These dogs are great if you're retired or work at home, and they make good traveling companions since they're easy to carry, don't take up much room in the car, and can fit beneath the seat on an airplane. Most breeders of toy dogs are wary of selling their pups to homes with very young children, but if your child is of an age to handle the dog carefully, a toy can make a great family pet. They are generally long-lived, bringing their families pleasure for 15 years or more.

TOY POODLE

It's no mystery why the Toy Poodle has maintained a high level of popularity for so many years. Smart as a whip and an excellent watchdog, this tiniest member of the Poodle trio is well suited to any size home and makes an ideal companion for someone who will enjoy keeping him company during the day. He's protective but not yappy, and is a quick learner who takes well to training, as evidenced by his history as a circus performer.

The Toy Poodle stands 10 inches or under at the shoulder, and his curly coat comes in a number of solid colors, including black, white, apricot, blue and brown. In addition to weekly nail, eye and ear care, daily combing and brushing is a must to maintain this dog's distinctive, elegant look. Unless the dog is kept in a short puppy clip, regular professional grooming may be necessary. To prevent infection, keep the ears clean and free of hair growth. Trimming the hair between the foot pads will keep mats from forming there. The Toy Poodle loves being pampered and is likely to bond to a single person. He prefers adults to small children. The breed's exercise needs are easily met with a couple of short walks each day, but be sure to provide him with toys or activities that will challenge his mind. Be aware of potential health problems such as luxating patellas (dislocating knees) and progressive retinal atrophy.

The Toy Poodle is well suited to any size home and makes an ideal companion for someone who will enjoy keeping her company during the day.

CHIHUAHUA

The Chihuahua's claim to fame is his status as the world's smallest dog, weighing in at two to six pounds. Some Chihuahuas grow a little larger, up to 12 pounds, but whatever their size, they make spirited, graceful, alert companions for people who want a dog they can take anywhere. The Chihuahua has a rounded skull with large, flaring ears and comes in two coat types, smooth and long, which may be any color.

The Chihuahua is the world's smallest dog. This is the long-coated variety.

A weekly brushing is all that's needed to keep this dog looking nice. Don't forget a sweater to keep the dog warm in cold weather. Chihuahuas don't need much exercise, but they become very attached to their people and won't be happy if left alone for long periods. They can be barky, but this trait makes them excellent watchdogs. With training, the Chihuahua can learn when to bark and when to keep quiet. Because of their diminutive size, Chihuahuas are usually not suited to homes with very young children, who don't have the motor skills or emotional maturity to handle them carefully. In the right home, however, they are a hardy, long-lived breed with personality to spare. Among the health problems that can affect Chihuahuas are patellar luxation, heart disease, hydrocephalus (water on the brain), juvenile hypoglycemia and collapsed trachea.

YORKSHIRE TERRIER

This is a lovely little toy dog with a lot of spirit and courage. The Yorkie is smart and independent, with a mind of its own. The combination of intelligence and terrier tenacity can make for a dog that is entertaining but stubborn. Yorkies want to please, but not if something more interesting comes along. This dog is still quite capable of carrying out his heritage as a ratter, sometimes amazing his owners, who were unaware of his predatory prowess. People who want a lap dog should consider a different breed, although the male Yorkie has a sweet temperament and enjoys sitting in a lap. Females are more likely to pick and choose when they want to be in your lap.

The Yorkshire Terrier is a feisty, elegant toy breed with a big-dog attitude who gets along well with other pets. Activities he's capable of participating in include obedience trials and agility. Potential health problems in the breed are patellar luxation, liver shunt, Legg-Perthes disease and tracheal collapse, as well as poor dental health if teeth aren't cared for. A daily session of grooming the fine, silky coat is a must, and it's time-consuming unless the dog is kept in a short clip. The Yorkie's color is a dark steel blue adorned with a rich golden tan headfall, chest and legs.

The Yorkie is a feisty, elegant toy breed who gets along well with other pets.

POMERANIAN

This dainty little dog is the smallest member of the spitz family and bears the characteristic profuse coat, pointed muzzle, prick ears and plumed tail carried over the back. In his homeland of Pomerania he was a

The Pomeranian is a curious, outgoing breed who wants to be friends with everyone he meets.

much larger dog, weighing up to 30 pounds, but 19th-century English breeders miniaturized him and made him the popular companion he is today.

Pomeranians weigh 3 to 7 pounds and come in numerous colors and patterns, including red, orange, cream, sable, black, brown, blue, black and tan, brindle, and particolor. The double coat needs gentle daily brushing to keep it free of mats. Curious and outgoing, the Pomeranian wants to be friends with everyone he meets. He's an excellent watchdog, barking to alert his people of anything unusual. He tends to bond to a single person and prefers adult companionship, ideally someone who will be home during the day to keep him company. His exercise needs are easily met with a couple of brief walks or playtimes each day. Patellar luxation is a potential health problem.

SHIH TZU

The Shih Tzu is a happy little dog who has been charming people for almost 2,000 years.

A product of the Chinese imperial court, the Shih Tzu is believed to have been charming people for almost 2,000 years. Its name (pronounced shidzoo) means "lion," but while the breed's dense, luxurious coat may appear leonine, its temperament is anything but. The

Shih Tzu is an outgoing, happy little dog who has a trusting, friendly attitude. Gentle but robust, he's capable of being a child's playmate or a loving companion to a more sedate older person. In general, the breed's health is good, although some dogs suffer from an inherited fatal kidney disorder. A drawback to the Shih Tzu is the daily grooming required to keep his long, elegant coat tangle-free. On the plus side, he doesn't shed much. He can be any color and is especially prized when he sports a white forehead blaze and tail tip.

The Shih Tzu is a toy breed, standing about 11 inches at the shoulder. He's definitely an indoor dog, not suited to life in a yard. As such, he's an excellent choice for people who live in apartments or condominiums. Despite his heritage, the Shih Tzu doesn't demand a palace and will be happy wherever he's loved.

MINIATURE PINSCHER

Often mistaken for a miniaturized version of the Doberman Pinscher, the Min Pin is a distinct breed that predates the Doberman by a couple of centuries. It was probably created through judicious crosses between the German smooth-haired Pinscher and perhaps the Italian Greyhound or the smooth Dachshund. He served as a capable ratter in the barnyard, but today his smart, lively personality and alert nature make him a popular pet and watchdog in any size home.

The Min Pin's smart, lively personality and alert nature make her a popular pet and watchdog in any size home.

Jaunty and sleek, moving with a high-stepping hackney gait, the Min Pin wears a short, smooth coat in red, black or brown, accented with rich tan markings. A weekly brushing keeps him looking slick. He stands 10 to 12½ inches at the shoulder, and his erect ears are usually cropped to a sharp point. Sturdy for his size, the Min Pin is a good playmate for older children, but he doesn't need a lot of exercise. A couple of short walks each day keep him happy. Patellar luxation is a potential health problem.

PUG

The Latin phrase *multum in parvo*—a big dog in a small body—is the perfect description of this breed. A mastiff in miniature, the Pug has been a favorite canine companion for centuries, thanks to his outgoing, charming disposition. The Dutch gave him the nickname of mopshond, meaning "to grumble," but behind that frowny face lies an affectionate, vivacious dog with a good sense of humor. Brought to Britain from Holland in the late 17th-century, the Pug probably came originally from China, where it may have been developed as a long-legged, smooth-coated variety of the Pekingese. Depending on your preference, the breed takes its name from *pugnus*, the Latin word for fist, or from the Old English word *pugg*, a term of endearment.

The Pug has been a favorite companion for centuries.

The compact Pug weighs 14 to 18 pounds and is sturdy and playful enough to be a child's companion. His short, fine coat is smooth and easy to care for with gentle weekly brushing. The coat comes in solid black or silver, or apricot-fawn with clearly defined dark markings forming a mask on the face. Large dark eyes and deep wrinkling on the forehead give the Pug an expression of concern. Check the eyes and head wrinkles regularly and clean them as needed. The calm, sedate Pug doesn't need a lot of exercise, but he is prone to obesity, so keep treats to a minimum. Heatstroke is a real concern for this short-faced dog, who should be kept in air-conditioned comfort when temperatures rise. The Pug snorts and snores, but otherwise he's not noisy.

MALTESE

This breed has been appreciated as a companion for three millennia. A Roman poet was so entranced by the dog that he extolled it as purer than a dove's kiss, gentler than a maiden and more precious than Indian gems. It's no wonder, for the Maltese has a sweet, affectionate manner combined with a sprightly, intelligent playfulness. An alert expression shines out of dark eyes, and the Maltese is an excellent watchdog, barking whenever anyone comes to the door. This breed tends to bond to a single person and prefers living with older children who will treat it carefully.

Draped in a mantle of silky white, the Maltese stands 10 inches at the shoulder and weighs 4 to 6 pounds. Daily combing and brushing keep the coat tangle-free, but it can be clipped to a shorter pet trim for easier maintenance. Whatever the length, frequent bathing is necessary to retain the coat's sparkling white-

Maltese are sweet, affectionate and playful.

ness. The Maltese doesn't need much exercise— indoor play or a brief walk will suit him just fine. As long as he's loved, he's happy living in any size accommodations.

PEKINGESE

Self-importance is a hallmark of the Peke personality, and no wonder. Created a thousand years ago in the Chinese imperial court, where they were prized as good luck charms, these richly coated toy dogs led pampered lives as noble pets, never setting paw outside palace walls. It was not until 1860, when British troops invaded the Summer Palace in Beijing and came upon five of the dogs guarding the body of their mistress, that the elegant little lion dogs became known to the

Western world. One of the captured dogs was pre-
sented to Queen Victoria, who named him Looty, as he
was a prize of war. These five Pekingese, plus a few others that were imported, were the foundation of the
modern Pekingese breed.

*With his family,
the Pekingese is
loving, loyal
and protective.*

The Pekingese weighs a maximum of 14 pounds, so
he's suited to any household, richly appointed or not.
The double coat comes in many colors and should be
brushed daily to keep it looking beautiful. Check eyes,
ears and nose wrinkles on a regular basis and clean
them as needed. True to his imperial heritage, the
Peke is not a "hail fellow, well met" kind of dog and is
rather standoffish toward strangers. With his family,
though, he's loyal and protective, not hesitating to
bark or show suspicion if a person or situation isn't to
his liking.

Like any dog, The Peke can be trained, but his stubborn nature will show itself if he doesn't want to do
something. Patient firmness will win the day. The
Pekingese doesn't need a lot of exercise and will be satisfied with a brief walk each day. Because his short muzzle makes him prone to heatstroke, he should be
protected from excessive temperatures. Young children won't find the Peke to be an active playmate, but
he could be a good choice for a quiet older child who's
interested in grooming and junior showmanship.

PAPILLON

Like the spread wings of a butterfly, the Papillon's fringed mobile ears sit at 45-degree angles atop his head. On some Papillons—who take their name from the French word for butterfly—a white blaze runs up the center of the forehead, heightening the butterfly resemblance. The Papillon was popular in European courts, and dogs of this type are often spotted in portraits by Rubens, Watteau, Fragonard and Boucher. Those early dogs usually had drop ears, though, a variety known as phalene that is still available today. Grace, beauty and a friendly nature make the Papillon a delightful companion for any home.

Even though he measures only 8 to 11 inches at the shoulder, he's a sturdy friend to older children and will happily join in games that aren't too rough. His exercise needs are easily met with a few brief walks or playtimes every day. The Papillon is easy to train, being intelligent and quick to learn. Some have even been trained to pull tiny carts and enjoy participating in parades and pet-assisted therapy at nursing homes and children's hospitals.

Elegance personified, the Papillon wears a long, fine, silky coat that can be white with patches of color from lemon to deep chestnut or black and white with tan markings. The look is topped off with a frill on the chest and a richly plumed tail that waves over the body. The Papillon doesn't shed much and is easily groomed with a weekly brushing and occasional bath. This is an affectionate dog that will prefer to have someone home during the day. Like so many toy breeds, the Papillon is alert to all comers and will bark when anyone approaches. Beware of letting this active little dog jump from high places; he may break a leg.

The Papillon gets her name from the fluttery appearance of her ears.

71

The Non-Sporting Group

Non-Sporting is a catchall term for a catchall gang of dogs. These are the breeds that didn't quite seem to fit in any other group, although a case could be made, perhaps, for placing the Standard Poodle and the Finnish Spitz in the Sporting Group or the Dalmatian in the Working Group. Most of these breeds serve primarily as companions, and very good at it they are. If you want a friendly, loving dog but desire something a little larger than the breeds in the Toy Group, this is the place to look. Because the Non-Sporting Group holds such a variety of dogs, it's difficult to generalize about them. Its members range from the small Boston Terrier and Bichon Frise to the large Standard Poodle and Dalmatian and lots of dogs in between. They come

in all coat types, colors and temperaments. Whether you choose a Non-Sporting breed or not will depend a lot on what you're looking for in a dog, but this group has something for everyone.

MINIATURE AND STANDARD POODLE

Miniature Poodle

Standard and Toy Poodles came along first, but it's the Miniature who is probably the most popular of the three. The Miniature Poodle stands at least 15 inches at the shoulder and is a smart, charming friend who's easy to train and quick to learn. Eager to please, he excels in obedience trials or anything else you might like to teach him.

The Mini adapts well to any accommodations, happy to parade through city streets or use his nose to sniff out truffles in the country.

The Miniature Poodle's pleasing personality and love for all family members makes him a good companion for young and old alike—as long as they're prepared to give him the grooming he needs. The Poodle doesn't shed much at all, but his thick curls need to be groomed regularly if he's to maintain his elegant look.

A short puppy clip is easier to care for than the highly stylized show clips that are vestiges of the Poodle's history as a water retriever.

Because Poodles are so popular, there are plenty of them around, but that doesn't negate the need to find a good breeder. This breed is prone to certain health problems, including progressive retinal atrophy and luxating patellas (dislocating knees) so be willing to wait for the right dog from the right person.

Standard Poodle

The oldest of the three Poodle varieties, the Standard was once used in Europe as a water retriever and is still capable of fulfilling that role today. The Standard Poodle wears an air of dignity and distinction, but deep down he's just a sweet, sociable, family-loving dog who enjoys playing with the kids and doubles as an excellent watchdog.

The Standard Poodle is the largest of the three Poodle varieties.

The Standard Poodle stands 22 to 26 inches at the shoulder and needs plenty of daily exercise to keep him occupied. The Poodle is a brainy breed and will find ways to entertain himself if you don't. He's highly trainable, though, and has a strong desire to please.

73

All Poodles have attitude, but this one has size to back it up. That, plus his good manners and intelligence, combine to make him a super companion for people who can give him the love and attention he needs. Those long, furry ears are prone to infection, so take special care to keep them clean and dry. Hip dysplasia can occur in this breed, so choose a breeder whose breeding stock is OFA-certified good or excellent.

The Boston Terrier is happiest when spending time with his people.

BOSTON TERRIER

A product of the American melting pot, the Boston Terrier was created from crosses between the English Terrier and the Bulldog. He's a smart, charming family dog who is easy to train and gets along well with kids and other pets. He likes being with his people, whatever they're doing, and an alert, observant nature makes him a great watchdog.

Boston Terriers come in three sizes: under 15 pounds, under 20 pounds and under 25 pounds. Even at 25 pounds, he's well suited to a home in the city. The breed's short, smooth coat—in brindle and white or the tuxedo look of black and white—needs only a weekly brushing to maintain its shine. The Boston's exercise needs are easily satisfied with a short daily walk. The Boston is healthy for the most part, but his prominent eyes are prone to injury. His short nose makes for a dog that snorts and snores, and may also predispose him to heat exhaustion or heatstroke.

BULLDOG

A symbol of courage and tenacity, the Bulldog earned his name and reputation in the cruel arenas of bull baiting and pit fighting. Happily, when those sports were outlawed as inhumane in 1835, the breed was rescued from extinction by dog lovers who recognized his admirable qualities. No longer aggressive, the modern Bulldog is prized for his sweet, smart and lovable personality. While the breed is moderately active in its youth, it mellows into a couch potato par excellence, although it will still enjoy a short daily walk or a brief play period.

In spite of their history of pit fighting, Bulldogs are a loveable breed.

Adult Bulldogs weigh 40 to 50 pounds and are well suited to life in the city or country. They learn quickly with positive reinforcement, and although not barky, their gruff appearance and determined nature makes them good watchdogs. When they're not relaxing, Bulldogs enjoy playing with the kids. On the down side, their snoring can keep you awake at night, and they tend to drool. Because of their short noses, Bulldogs are prone to heatstroke and heat exhaustion and need special care during the summer. The short, fine coat sheds heavily, but a weekly brushing is all that's needed to remove dead hair.

BICHON FRISE

Cheerful and animated, this breed has been known since the 14th century, when it was a favorite pet of the aristocratic set. Fashions changed, however, and the little Bichon Teneriffe, as it was then known, found itself on the streets. Fortunately, the dogs' sweetness ensured their survival, and in the 1930s they officially became recognized as a breed under the new name Bichon Frise, meaning curly-coated lap dog, a perfect description of this delightful breed.

The Bichon's size—12 inches or less at the shoulder—makes him ideally suited to any size home. He likes children and makes a good watchdog. A daily walk is nice, but he doesn't need a lot of exercise. His large

dark eyes shine with intelligence, and his curly white coat doesn't shed much. On the down side, a Bichon needs frequent bathing and daily brushing to maintain that spiffy look. People with little time to spare should consider regular professional grooming for this breed. Bichons can also be difficult to housetrain, so be patient and keep plenty of stain and odor remover on hand. With the right owner, though, their winning ways can overcome those drawbacks.

The Bichon Frise is a charming, animated little companion.

The sturdy little Lhasa Apso is naturally intelligent and alert.

LHASA APSO

Originally serving as a palace watchdog in Tibet, this sturdy little breed is naturally alert, with sharp hearing and intelligence that make him a wonderful companion, suited to life in any size home. He's suspicious of strangers—more so on his home turf—and tends to bond to a single person, although he'll be devoted to the entire family. Homes with children are fine, as long as they are old enough to treat him with respect.

Lhasas are thinkers, and they like to examine people and situations thoroughly before accepting them. An older Lhasa being adopted into a new home may take some time to adjust, but most likely he'll come around. Beneath a calm exterior, the Lhasa can be stubborn and independent, so patient training is necessary without being harsh or strict.

This breed reaches full maturity at 3 or 4 years of age and remains young at heart into their teens. The Lhasa has a long, dense coat that requires daily maintenance to avoid becoming a matted mess. These dogs like to be clean, so don't let grooming chores slide. Or consider keeping the coat clipped short for easier upkeep. In full coat, however, the Lhasa has a regal bearing that reflects his palace past.

DALMATIAN

For long-distance joggers and other athletic types, the Dalmatian hits the spot. A heritage as a carriage dog, fire wagon escort, ratter and circus performer makes this elegant and distinctive breed ideal for people with lots of time and energy to spend with a dog. Dalmatians

Even though Dalmations are "on-the-go" dogs, they take time out to cuddle with their people.

have an affinity for horses, so they're especially at home on farms, ranches and country estates, but they can adapt to any environment where their exercise needs are met.

This is a large breed that stands 19 to 23 inches at the shoulder, and its reserved and protective nature makes it a good watchdog. The Dalmatian is a favorite choice of children who have seen the animated or live-action films *101 Dalmatians*, but parents of small children should keep in mind that the Dal is a high-energy animal that can be too much dog for a toddler.

Clad in a short, glossy coat, the Dalmatian is born white, with the black or liver spots developing later. A Dalmatian with a patch won't make it in the show ring, but that doesn't disqualify him from being a great companion. Shedding isn't excessive, and a good brushing with a hound glove about three times a week keeps the coat shiny. Deafness is a concern in this breed, so be sure the breeder you buy from tests her breeding stock and puppies for hearing ability.

CHINESE SHAR-PEI

In the early 1970s, the Chinese Shar-Pei teetered on the brink of extinction, but just 20 years later it is one of the most popular AKC-registered breeds. With a head like a hippo, a blue-black tongue, tiny ears, and wrinkly skin that makes puppies look as if they're parading around in their parents' clothes, the breed's unusual appearance is an appealing factor to many would-be buyers.

The Chinese Shar-Pei is a strong, independent breed that likes to bond with a single family member.

However, the Chinese Shar-Pei is a lot more than a cute bundle of wrinkles (which disappear on the body as the dog matures and fills out the skin). This is a strong, independent breed that tends to bond to a single person. An aloof nature makes him wary of strangers, and he's fiercely protective of his home and family. Without good early socialization and firm, consistent training, the Chinese Shar-Pei can be aggressive toward people or other animals. He has a moderate activity level and doesn't demand a huge amount of exercise, although he'll appreciate a couple of daily walks. Grooming is easy, with the short, solid-colored coat requiring only a weekly brushing. Potential health concerns include entropion, in which the eyelid turns inward, and skin problems.

CHOW CHOW

The Chow Chow is noted for his teddy bear appearance, blue-black tongue, and a curious stilted walk caused by a lack of angulation in the lower joint of the hind legs. A member of the spitz family, the breed originated in China where it guarded property, hunted and pulled carts. The Chow Chow made his way out of China in the 19th century and gained popularity when noted dog lover Queen Victoria took an interest in him.

The independent Chow Chow is a one-person dog, stubborn and prone to aggression if he doesn't receive plenty of early socialization combined with firm, consistent training. Because he's suspicious of strangers, he makes a good watchdog. The breed's pride is its luxuriant, offstanding coat in solid colors of red, black, tawny, blue or cream. Shedding is heavy, and the coat should be brushed about three times a week to keep the hair under control. A smooth-coated variety offers a little less hair to deal with. This powerful dog, which weighs up to 55 pounds, will enjoy regular outdoor exercise, but his activity level isn't excessive. When he's not standing guard, he makes a fine TV-watching companion. Entropion is a potential health problem.

Chow Chows make wonderful watchdogs because they are suspicious of strangers.

The Herding Group

The Nitty Gritty

Like the working breeds, herding dogs are also serious about their work. They were developed to herd flocks using "eye," a controlling gaze, or by nipping at the heels of stock to get them to move in the right direction. Naturally, a herding breed has lots of energy, since it was bred to work hard all day long. So, be prepared to keep one of these dogs busy. They like to have a job, and whatever it is, they'll do it well. Herding breeds are major proponents of family togetherness, since they like to have all the members of their "flock" together. Don't be surprised if they try to herd the kids or the cats. Herding breeds are good family dogs if they're given enough exercise and training. They love children and will protect them to the best of their ability. Some of them can be nippy, however, not out of meanness, but simply because they're trying to direct you or another family member to wherever it is they want you to be. A trainer can help you discourage and redirect this behavior.

German Shepherd Dogs are one of the smartest, most versatile breeds of dogs.

GERMAN SHEPHERD DOG

"The look of eagles" is how proud German Shepherd owners describe their dogs' noble appearance, the strong and muscular body and the subtle but unmistakable steadiness of character that embodies the family motto of the man who helped created the breed: "Do right and fear no one." Captain Max von Stephanitz started in the 1890s with German farm dogs and molded them into his vision of an elegant yet versatile herding breed. Returning servicemen brought the dogs to the United States after World War I, and one of those dogs became Rin Tin Tin, the heroic star of the silver screen. His exciting exploits boosted the breed's popularity into the stratosphere. The breed's versatility also made it sought after for police and military work and as a guide dog.

Today, the German Shepherd Dog ranks among the AKC's 10 most popular, and for good reason. This intelligent, loyal breed is devoted to its family, especially children, and is an outstanding guard dog, willing and able to protect his people from all comers. He responds well to training, which should begin with puppy kindergarten at 10 to 12 weeks of age, and is frequently found participating in obedience trials and other dog sports.

This is a large breed, with males standing 25 inches at the shoulder and weighing 75 to 80 pounds. Females are on the smaller side. The German Shepherd adapts to its family's environment and activity level, but it's a good idea for this dog to feel as if he has a job to do, so keep him busy with training, play and involvement in family life. Sadly, many German Shepherds are prone to debilitating hip dysplasia, so choose your breeder carefully, looking for one that x-rays breeding stock to ensure excellent hip condition. Because of this, put off training that involves jumping until the dog is about two years old, and take steps to make sure he doesn't become overweight. The German Shepherd also sheds heavily, so be prepared to thoroughly brush the dense double coat on a regular basis. The most familiar German Shepherd look is black and tan, but this breed also comes in black or varying shades of sable.

SHETLAND SHEEPDOG

Often referred to as a miniature Collie, the Shetland Sheepdog is a breed unto itself, and its fanciers sometimes jokingly call it "the un-Collie." Originating in the harsh environs of the Shetland Islands, off Scotland's northeast coast, the Sheltie was a farm dog, whose job it was to herd the diminutive flocks found on the islands. He was nicknamed the "toonie," a name taken from the Norwegian word "tun," meaning farm.

Eventually the toonie made his way from island farm to mainland and made his dog show debut in 1906 at Crufts, the famous British show. There, he appeared under the name Shetland Collie, but after Collie breeders objected the name was changed to Shetland Sheepdog. Smart and easy to train, the modern Sheltie

Although some people may think of the Sheltie as a small Collie, Shetland Sheepdogs are truly their own unique breed.

has made a name for himself as one of the top breeds in obedience trials, and these characteristics make him a popular family pet as well.

Standing 13 to 16 inches at the shoulder, the Sheltie fits in any size home; however, his habit of barking can make him unsuited to apartment life unless someone will be with him during the day. On the other hand, this makes him an excellent watchdog. He's highly active and will appreciate a couple of good walks each day. An owner who takes him jogging or runs him alongside a bicycle can also give him the exercise he needs. His level of activity and sweet disposition make him a good playmate for kids. The Sheltie has a dense double coat that may be black, blue merle or sable marked with white and/or tan. It sheds heavily and should be brushed thoroughly at least three times a week.

COLLIE

Kind, loyal, and smart, the Collie may well be the Boy Scout of dogdom. The most famous Collie, of course, was Lassie, who brought these traits to life in books, television and movies and is still popular today for her cleverness and bravery. The Collie is a breed of Scottish origin and was invaluable to shepherds for its ability to round up flocks and drive them to market.

Like so many breeds, the Collie was brought to the public eye through the interest of Queen Victoria, who encountered the dogs while vacationing at her Highland home of Balmoral. The most well-known Collie is the rough coat, but many people don't know that the breed also comes in a smooth variety. In either variety, the coat may be sable and white, tri-color, blue merle or white. Expect to brush the rough coat frequently to remove dead hair and prevent mats from forming. The smooth coat can get by with weekly brushing. Both varieties are subject to heavy seasonal shedding.

The Collie stands 22 to 26 inches at the shoulder and weighs 50 to 75 pounds.

The Collie is known for her cleverness, bravery and loyalty.

Although it's somewhat large, it can adapt to smaller homes as long as it's provided with daily exercise. Beloved of children and grown-ups alike, the Collie is a fine family watchdog and companion who will be satisfied with moderate amounts of activity and lots of loving attention.

PEMBROKE WELSH CORGI

This is the Corgi without a tail, but nonetheless a member of the spitz family, as evidenced by his prick ears and wedge-shaped head. The progenitors of the Pembroke Welsh Corgi most likely came to England in the 12th century in the company of Flemish weavers, who were brought over to help develop cloth manufacture. The little dogs soon became part of the warp and woof of Wales, especially Pembrokeshire, where the weavers settled, and became highly valued as drover dogs, herding sheep and cattle down the narrow lanes to market.

The word corgi can be translated as "working dog" or "dwarf dog" and was probably applied to any small working dog. Although he shares the name with the Cardigan Welsh Corgi, the two are separate breeds, with the Cardigan believed to have Dachshund rather than spitz ancestry. The Pembroke has always been the more popular of the two, the more so after it received royal favor, with Rozavel Golden Eagle becoming the special pet of young Princess Elizabeth, one day to become Queen Elizabeth II. She still keeps Corgis to this day. Alert and vigilant, the Pembroke is an excellent watchdog who loves children. He's not shy about expressing his interest in and affection toward people, but he doesn't force himself on them. His medium-long coat comes in red, sable, fawn, or black

Although there are two breeds with the name Corgi, the Pembroke Welsh Corgi is more popular than the Cardigan Welsh Corgi.

and tan, with or without white markings. A good brushing three times a week will keep it shiny and clean. This breed does shed heavily on a seasonal basis, so be prepared for flying hair.

The Pembroke is small, standing 10 to 12 inches at the shoulder, so he fits well into any home where the family is willing to exercise him daily. He's smart, with a sense of humor, so be on your toes when dealing with him.

AUSTRALIAN SHEPHERD

Despite his name, the Australian Shepherd was made in the U.S.A., where he's been used for more than a century to herd sheep and other livestock. Besides being a talented stockdog, the Australian Shepherd has found a place in the American home, where he serves double duty as a children's playmate and a watchdog. He barks ferociously whenever anyone dares to approach his house or even walk by on the sidewalk. The Aussie has many good qualities, but he's a brainy breed that requires early, consistent training. Without it, he'll soon be running the show. When his intelligence is properly channeled, though, this breed can learn to do just about anything.

This is a medium-size dog with a coat that comes in blue merle, black, red merle or red, all with or without white or tan markings. The Aussie is a heavy shedder and needs weekly brushing to keep its medium-length coat tangle-free. Unless he was born with a natural bobtail, his tail is docked when he's about three days old. Keep this dog busy and well exercised, and he'll make a wonderful companion.

The Australian Shepherd is a brainy playmate and affectionate watchdog.

5

Researching Breeds

A Cocker Spaniel and Golden Retriever

Now that you have an idea of what some of the breeds are like, it's time to do some in-depth research to make sure the one you've chosen is really right for you or to learn about some of the many other dog breeds that weren't covered in the previous chapter. You can find out more about a particular breed by reading books, searching the Internet, contacting the breed club, talking to people who own the breed, attending a dog show and dog sitting.

Publications

Your first stop should be the library, a bookstore, or a pet store with a good supply of breed books. The reference librarian can direct you to the shelves where pet books are kept, and most bookstores and pet stores have pet book sections. If you're starting your search at the library, make sure the books you choose are fairly up-to-date, published within the last three to five years. You want to be sure you have the most current information about the breed's health and temperament, after all.

Keep in mind that not all breed books are created equal. Some are aimed at breeders and exhibitors and don't contain much of interest to the person who wants a pet. These books are full of show photos and information about the breed's history in various countries or the people who were influential in the breed's development, but are less helpful when it comes to information about what the dog is like to live with or how she should be trained. Many publishers have stepped in, however, with books that are meant to serve as guides for new dog owners. These books discuss a breed's history in relation to its qualifications as a pet; go into great detail about temperament or personality, how well the dog gets along with children or other pets, and how it should be trained; and cover health issues that affect the breed, which the buyer should be aware of. Look at two or three of these books to make sure you get a well-rounded picture of the breed.

Dog magazines frequently publish profiles of breeds. Look on the newsstand for one that's featuring a breed you're interested in, or search back issues at the library.

Surfing the Web

The Internet is another good source of information. The American Kennel Club has an extensive Web site with articles on finding a breeder and buying a puppy as well as information about all the breeds it registers, parent club addresses and contact names, and links to national clubs that have Web pages of their own. Many breed clubs have Web pages devoted to their breed, on which you can find the breed standard, history of the breed, contacts for breeders or rescue groups, and

The Internet provides a growing community of dog lovers from all over the world. (Pomeranian)

links to other pages about the breed, from people around the world. A number of foreign Web pages are written in English, and it can be fun to compare their breed information with that provided on U.S. or Canadian Web pages.

Lots of breeders create Web pages with pictures of their dogs, notices of puppy availability, and sometimes articles they've written about caring for or training their dogs. Even if a breeder's Web page seems complete, you'll still want to talk to him or her—in person, if possible—to get a feel for his knowledge of and care for his dogs.

Breed rescue organizations have a Web presence as well. These groups rescue and place homeless purebreds, and they're an excellent resource if you want a purebred but like the idea of saving a life. Learn more about breed rescue groups in chapter 9.

Other Web sites are devoted to dog care in general. They include detailed discussions of the responsibilities of dog ownership, information on choosing a dog, questions you should ask yourself before entering into dog ownership, profiles of specific breeds, the right dog for apartment or condo living, and advice on successfully integrating a dog into your home, including introducing a new dog to other pets. A number of recommended sites are listed in chapter 11.

Another great Internet resource is the large number of mailing lists devoted to different breeds. A mailing list is sort of like a round robin letter for breed enthusiasts, only by e-mail. Most mailing lists permit anyone to join, although some are by invitation only. Once you join, you can introduce yourself and let other members know that you're interested in learning more about their breed. They'll most likely be glad to share their knowledge with you. You'll also see messages from people about behavior or health problems they've had with their dogs, reasons why they love their dogs, activities they do with their dogs, experiences traveling with them, and numerous—sometimes hot and heavy—discussions on nutrition, health, breeding, spaying/neutering, training, showing and much more. All of this information will help you make the right decision about whether to acquire that breed.

Besides breed-specific mailing lists, there are lists devoted simply to dogs in general. You'll want to join one of these if you're considering getting a mixed breed or just want information on what it's like to live with a dog, any dog.

To learn how to find and join a mailing list, see chapter 11. Mailing lists have strict rules about how to post to them and what types of language and discussion are permissible, so be sure to carefully read the introductory information you'll receive when you join.

Sometimes talking to a friend who owns the breed that you are investigating is the best way to get information. (Australian Shepherds)

Personal Interviews

One of the best ways to learn about a breed is by word of mouth. Do you have friends or neighbors who have the kind of dog you're interested in? Pick their brains about why they chose her, whether they'd choose her again, where they got her, what health problems she's had, and what she's like to live with—the good and the bad. You may be surprised at some of the things you learn.

Your veterinarian may also have some experience with the breed you're interested in. He can tell you whether the ones he's seen have been generally healthy and temperamentally sound. He may even be able to refer you to a breeder who produces good-quality dogs.

Talking to breeders should be your next step. An established breeder with a lot of love for the breed can be an invaluable resource when you're trying to decide whether to acquire a certain type of dog. She can help you evaluate your lifestyle, home environment and family needs and tell you whether her breed would be a good choice for you. A caring breeder wants only the best for the breed and will tell you honestly if she thinks it's not right for you, and why. You can find breeders through recommendations from the national or regional breed club, on the Internet, as mentioned previously, and at dog shows.

Many breeds have a parent club that can provide you with information on the dogs. (Cavalier King Charles Spaniel)

Breed Clubs

If you're interested in a particular breed, contact the parent club for information. Breed clubs usually have packets of information, including breeder referrals, available to interested buyers. It's expensive to put together such packets, so the club may charge you a small fee for the packet or ask you to send a self-addressed stamped envelope to cover postage and handling.

The national club is also a good resource for locating breeders. Clubs usually have a board member who's designated as the breeder referral secretary or some similar title. This person can refer you to club members in your area and nationwide. In general, club members are required to subscribe to a code of ethics, so that's why you should start your search with the national club. Sad to say, not everyone who subscribes to a code of ethics lives up to it, so you'll want to use your common sense when interviewing them and inspecting their kennels and dogs. Don't just assume that a club member is automatically an ethical breeder.

Dog Shows

Besides being a good venue for talking to breeders, a dog show is an opportunity for you and your family to see lots of different dogs, all at one time. Reading about them is one thing, but seeing them in the flesh is quite another. Unless you're already familiar with them, you might not have realized exactly how large a Great Dane is or how tiny a Toy Poodle is.

Get to the dog show early so you can buy a catalog and find out where and when the breed you're interested in

Dog shows often include many different breeds. They are a good venue at which to talk to breeders. (Golden Retriever)

will be shown. Most dog shows begin at 8 a.m. and unless the show is benched—meaning that the dogs must be on exhibit if they're not in the ring—most exhibitors leave as soon as their class is over, unless they've won, of course, and are advancing to the next class. Very few shows are benched these days—an exception is the Westminster Kennel Club show, held every February in New York City at Madison Square Garden—so don't count on your breed being there all day. Scout out breeders, introduce yourself, and ask if they have time to talk to you after they're finished showing. Most breeders are happy to talk about their dogs and share their experiences with them, but before showing, they'll be busy grooming their dogs

91

and psyching themselves up for the competition, so
that's not a good time to start peppering them with
questions.

You'll meet breeders who live in your area, plus some
from out of town. When you talk to breeders at the
show, tell them a little bit about yourself and why you're
interested in their breed. Talk to
several breeders so you can get a
good, all-around picture of the
breed. If breeders are local, you may
be able to set up a time to interview
them further at their home and
meet more of their dogs. A breeder
who lives in your area may want to
inspect your home as well to make
sure you have a securely fenced yard
and suitable living area for the
breed in question.

A breeder may or may not have
puppies available at the time that
you're looking, but it's still a good
idea to get to know her and her
dogs, to make sure she's someone
you want to deal with in the future.
If she's not planning a litter for a
while, she can probably refer you to another breeder.
Now that you've gathered all this information and are
sure about your choice, you can begin your search for
a puppy in earnest.

WHAT'S A BREED CLUB?

A national breed club, or parent
club, represents a particular breed.
A club's purpose is to promote,
protect and present its breed to the
public. The national club is responsible for drafting and revising the
breed standard, holding at least
one annual national specialty show
(which showcases only that particular breed), and supporting the
regional and local specialty clubs
throughout the country. National
clubs often sponsor judges education seminars, and support breed
rescue and research into health
problems that face their breed, so
they're an important resource for
owners of purebred dogs.

Dog Sitting

Dog sitting, whether for pay or free of charge, is
another excellent way to find out if a certain breed is
to your liking. Keep in mind that the dog you are taking care of is bound to be nervous and uncertain without her owner nearby. So don't judge too harshly if
your charge paces or barks or even seems frightened of
you at first. These are normal reactions, and not
necessarily a reflection of the breed that you are dog
sitting. Give her time to settle down and then get ready
to take some notes.

It is always a good idea to get to know the dog that you will be watching before her owner leaves town. A Saturday or Sunday afternoon might seem like the best option to you, but if pooch and her companion regularly take evening walks together after a long workday apart, you might want to join in then. In this way, the dog can get to know you in neutral territory—and you can get to know the dog within her normal routine. This jaunt will also clue you in to the dog's favorite activities—does she like to fetch? Or is Frisbee more to her liking? On the other hand, if this dog is a couch potato, you may not discover it until you are both curled up together at night watching television.

Conversely, you may also discover that this dog needs a lot more exercise and attention than you are able to provide even for a short duration of time. In this case, it is best to bow out gracefully, and early, preferably before your dog-sitting adventure begins. You certainly do not want an anxious owner coming home from a trip to find both dog and dog sitter suffering through each other's company.

If you decide to dog sit, it is a good idea to be prepared. Make sure to bring clothes that you don't mind getting full of dog hair or dog slobber. Have enough food on hand for both yourself and your charge. Then, once you are settled in, invite a few conscientious friends over. You are sure to quickly discover a few significant details. Does this dog bark incessantly? Is she friendly or timid? Does she like to play or does she run away from people? Sometimes dogs just aren't properly socialized—this is another issue entirely—but "bad behavior" may be an indication that a particular breed is just not for you. If you are dog sitting a terrier, for instance, and you have a retiring personality, you will soon realize that you don't have the energy to spend with this type of dog. Alternatively, hanging out with a Bulldog will seem like a breeze. Always keep in mind that just like people, dogs are individuals with personalities of their own.

part three

Commitment Time

chapter 6

What to Look For in a Breeder

(Pembroke Welsh Corgis)

People who breed dogs are a dime a dozen, but the really good ones are worth their weight in gold. A good breeder is knowledgeable about and experienced in his breed, is passionate about it, wants only the best for it and gives his dogs the best health care and nutrition that money can buy. He belongs to one or more breed clubs, usually the national club and a local or regional club, and abides by the club's code of ethics. He titles his dogs in conformation shows and may put working titles on them as well. A dog that can perform well in the show ring and still do the work for which she was created is a rare animal indeed.

What Is a Good Breeder?

Good breeders are dedicated to their dogs, realizing that there's always something new to learn, and working to maintain and improve the breed. With that in mind, they prepare long-term breeding plans that take into account which matings will be most likely to produce dogs with sound health, temperament and appearance. When they breed a litter, they're prepared to keep all the puppies for as long as it takes to place them in loving, appropriate homes. For that reason, they often don't breed until they have a waiting list of approved people who have paid a deposit for one of their next puppies.

You're probably wondering why it's important to buy from a show breeder when all you want is a family pet. Keep in mind that a dog show is meant to be more than just a beauty pageant. Show dogs are the results of an exhibitor's breeding program, brought out so they can be evaluated by qualified judges as well as other breeders. Someone who exhibits his dogs must be committed to a painstaking breeding plan that incorporates good conformation, sound health and temperament, meticulous grooming, and excellent nutrition. He must invest in high-quality food and regular veterinary care.

What Does a Good Breeder Do?

In addition to good nutrition, and regular vaccinations and deworming, breeders face other veterinary costs as well. Before breeding, dogs should be tested for brucellosis—a sexually transmitted disease—and receive a physical exam that focuses on their readiness for breeding and identifies potential problems such as a narrow pelvis. A sperm count is often done for unproven stud dogs, older dogs, or those that haven't sired a litter in a while. Both dogs must be parasite-free and up-to-date on their vaccinations. In addition, there's the process of testing breeding stock for genetic disorders so diseases won't be passed on to pups. Among the tests a breeder might have done are a thyroid panel, eye exam, and hip or elbow x-rays. Run, don't walk, away from any breeder who says that genetic testing is worthless or that his lines don't have any problems. An honest breeder will tell you otherwise.

Puppies from a good breeder will have lots of human contact and socialization. (Pointers)

Good breeders also spend lots of time socializing their litters by getting the pups used to all kinds of people, places, sounds, noises and smells at an early age. Their ultimate goal is to produce dogs that shine with health and happiness.

Besides breed club membership and involvement in pertinent sports or other activities, a good breeder is identified by length of time in the breed, indicating a strong commitment to it. He has owned, exhibited and bred dogs of a particular breed for at least five years. There's nothing wrong with a breeder who doesn't have this much longevity—everyone has to start somewhere—but in most cases he works closely with a more experienced mentor.

It may not mean much to you that a pup's parents have earned championships or have been tested for genetic problems before being bred, especially if you just want a dog to pal around with. But look at it from a long-term point of view: A large part of your pup's future health and temperament depends on how good a start she had in life. When you buy a car, you don't go out and plunk down your hard-earned money for just any old clunker—you read *Consumer Reports* and *Motor Trend* to find one that's well built and reliable, and you buy from a dealer who stands behind his product. The same should be true when you buy a purebred dog.

Visiting a Breeder's Home

Once you have the names of a few breeders, it's time to start setting up interviews. It's always best if you can talk to a breeder at his home so you can see how and where his dogs are raised. Puppies should be brought up in a clean, stimulating home environment, where they're exposed to such typical aspects of home life as kids or cats, the sounds of the doorbell, vacuum cleaner, washer and dryer, television and the good smells emanating from the kitchen. A puppy that has been raised in a home environment is more likely to adjust easily to your home.

Visiting the breeder in person is the best way to determine what the puppy's home-life has been like since birth. (Papillon)

Anyone who lives with a number of dogs probably isn't going to win the Good Housekeeping Clean Home of the Year award, but a breeder's house and kennel facilities should be reasonably clean and well kept, with feces picked up regularly to keep down odor and possible trans-mission of diseases and parasites. A breeder who doesn't permit home visits may have something to hide, such as unsanitary conditions or excessive numbers of dogs. Cross this person off your list, and move on to someone else.

After you've arrived and chit-chatted for a while, the breeder will introduce you to his dogs, if they haven't come sniffing around already. Some breeders will let the whole gang out to greet you, to get an idea of how you react to dogs, while others will just show you the mom and puppies.

Being able to meet the pups' mother is a real plus. She has a major influence on puppy temperament. You can look at her and have a very good idea of how your puppy will look and act at maturity. Socialization is a factor, too, of course, but in general, a happy, confident mother is likely to produce happy, confident puppies, and a nervous, shy mother is likely to produce nervous, shy puppies.

Even if you are not able to meet the father of the litter, you may be able to see pictures or a video of him. (Basset Hound)

The pups' father probably won't be on the premises, but you can ask to see photos or videos of him. If he's local, though, you may want to visit his owner as well so you can get a better idea of his temperament and looks. Ask the breeder why he chose to breed to that particular dog and what qualities he seems to have contributed to the litter. Both parents should be at least

two years old. Any younger than that, they aren't fully mature. Also, some health certifications, such as OFA ratings of hips and elbows, can't be done before two years of age.

Speaking of health certifications, ask the breeder what pre-breeding tests he had performed. From your research, you should already have an idea of what problems can affect the breed. Depending on the breed, you can expect to see OFA ratings for hips, elbows or patellas, results from ultrasounds or electrocardiograms showing that the heart is healthy, or CERF reports showing that the eyes are clear of progressive retinal atrophy, cataracts or other hereditary diseases.

Because he's invested so much time and effort into his puppies, a breeder rightly views them as the future of the breed and screens potential buyers carefully to make sure they're right for the breed and able to provide loving, responsible ownership.

Twenty Questions

Asking questions is how you and the breeder get to know one another. Don't be shy or feel as if you're being nosey. You're putting a large chunk of money down on a long-term investment, and you have a right to know what you're paying for. Conversely, the breeder has a right to know what kind of home and family he's sending his precious puppies to, and he'll question you just as thoroughly. The following questions are things you should ask the breeder. In the next section, you'll find a list of things he's likely to ask you.

YOUR QUESTIONS

Are you a member of national and local breed clubs? Breed club membership shows a commitment to the betterment of the breed. Breed club involvement, such as serving on a committee or as an officer, shows that the breeder is respected by his peers.

How many years have you been involved with this breed? Again, length of time in a breed shows commitment to it. It can be an indicator that the person you're dealing with isn't just a fly-by-night breeder hoping to capitalize on a particular breed's fleeting popularity.

How many litters have you bred? Experience is good, but more is not necessarily better. Most breeders plan a litter only once every couple of years, when they have the right dogs and a list of potential buyers with whom they can place any puppies they choose not to keep and exhibit.

It is not rude or inappropriate for you to ask a few questions of the breeder. (Chihuahua)

What are the most serious health problems found in this breed? You should have an idea of these problems from your research. Expect a good breeder to elaborate on them for you and to discuss what the breed as a whole and the breeder in particular are doing to address the problems.

How is your breeding program addressing those problems? Screening for disease before breeding and choosing stud dogs for their sound health as well as conformation and temperament are ways to prevent problems. A breeder who claims to have "just been lucky" probably isn't someone you want to deal with.

What temperament or behavior problems might this breed have? Some breeds are prone to shyness or aggression, others tend to be barkers or chewers. The breeder should prepare you for any problems you might encounter and offer advice on how to deal with it. A good breeder is willing to be there for you throughout the dog's life, to help you with any problems you might face.

Can you provide references from other people who have bought puppies from you? Most breeders will be happy to give you the names of other people who have purchased puppies from them. Don't just take the names; call the people and find out if they're happy with their dog and whether they would buy from the breeder again.

THE BREEDER'S QUESTIONS

Be prepared to answer the following questions from breeders. They're not being nosey; they just want to be sure their pups go to appropriate homes where they'll be loved for a lifetime.

What made you decide to get this particular breed? Explain why your personality and lifestyle make this breed a good choice for you.

Are you familiar with the breed's characteristics? Discuss the research you've done about the breed and why it appeals to you.

Have you owned a dog before? If yes, do you still have it; if no, why not? Some breeds are not really suited to novice dog owners, and the breeder wants to make sure you'll be able to handle the dog appropriately and that your current dog is going to get along with this particular breed.

Do you own or rent your home? If you rent, are pets permitted? Even if you own your home, some homeowners associations limit the number or type of pets a family can have, as do most apartment complexes. You're not really going to be able to sneak this particular breed in and out every day, so the breeder wants to make sure you'll truly be able to have the dog in your current home.

It's also acceptable and even expected for a breeder to ask you some questions about yourself and your lifestyle. Don't worry, it's all a customary part of the process. (Border Collie)

Do you have a fenced yard? If you don't, how do you plan to handle a dog's elimination needs? If you plan for your dog to spend part of her time outdoors, you need a securely fenced yard to keep her from roaming or being stolen. Condo or apartment dwellers might not have a yard, but they still need to have access to a common area or nearby park where the dog can exercise and eliminate.

Will the dog spend most of her time indoors or outdoors? When she's outdoors, what kind of shelter will she have from heat and cold? It's okay for a dog to spend time outdoors, but her whole life shouldn't be limited to the backyard. When she is there, however, will she have a sturdy doghouse, a shaded area and access to plenty of fresh water?

How much time do you have to spend with a dog? Without social contact, dogs are more likely to develop behavior problems, which in turn makes their people not want to spend time with them. The breeder doesn't want this to happen to one of his puppies.

103

Are you prepared to give this particular breed plenty of training and exercise? All dogs of any size, purebred or mixed breed, need training and exercise. Training makes them nice to live with, and exercise keeps them physically and mentally healthy.

Do you have children? How old are they? Infants and toddlers aren't old enough to safely interact with a dog without close supervision. Toy breeds are at risk of injury if they're mishandled by a youngster. And, any dog can bite if she's pushed far enough. Consider carefully whether your child is old enough for a dog, has a real interest in a dog, and whether you have the time to provide the necessary supervision and education that both will need to become best friends.

Do you plan to spay or neuter the dog at the appropriate age? There are many millions more dogs (and cats) than there are homes available for them. The good breeder wants to ensure that his puppies don't contribute to the overpopulation problem and will require you to spay or neuter a dog that will simply be a pet. This is good for the health of the dog and for the health of the dog population as a whole.

chapter 7

Pick
of the
Litter

When you've found some breeders you like and trust, the hard part of finding a dog is over and the fun part begins: looking at litters and choosing from among the puppies. As you cuddle each cute baby, her big dark eyes stare trustingly into yours with an expression that seems to say "Take me home."

(Labrador Retrievers)

Before you fall for the first puppy you see, though, it's a good idea to have decided ahead of time which sex you want, whether you prefer a specific color or pattern, and whether you want a pet or a show dog. You can also perform temperament tests that will help you decide which pup best suits your personality and needs.

Boy or Girl?

Other than size, there isn't usually a tremendous difference between male and female dogs. Everyone has preferences, though, based on their own experiences. Dogs are individuals, and what is true of one may not be the case at all with the next. Ask the breeder what sex-related differences he has noticed in the breed. Sometimes females are said to be more protective or more focused. Oftentimes they are quieter or more docile than males. Males can have more of a sense of humor and may be more loving or attentive toward their people.

Color

The development of various coat colors in dogs was a by-product of domestication, a result of artificial selection. According to experimental evidence, color and temperament seemed to be linked in many domestic animals. The first domestic dogs were a sort of yellowish tan, a color still seen in dingos today, and it may have been that small, light-colored dogs were more manageable than those with a more wolfish appearance.

A good dog is never a bad color. (Belgian Tervuren and Bichon Frise)

In some breeds today, people claim that different colors have different temperaments. For instance, particolored Cocker Spaniels are said to be "busier" than buffs and blacks, which are pegged as easygoing. Black-and-tan Cockers are supposed to be the thinkers of the Cocker varieties, smart and trainable. Black-and-white particolors tend to have clownish personalities, while red-and-whites tend to be more loving and affectionate. Of course, those are just the opinions of a few Cocker owners, and others may have had entirely different experiences. Choose your puppy based on what you and the breeder see in her, not on what might be true of some other dog.

In most cases, the color of your dog isn't really important, except as a matter of personal preference. To paraphrase an old saying: A good dog is never a bad color.

Personality and Working Ability

As you look over all the puppies, keep in mind what you're looking for in a dog beyond appearance or sex. If you want a lap dog, go for the puppy that snuggles comfortably into your arms instead of wriggling to get free. If you want a dog with a good nose, that will perform well in scent-related sports or activities, look for the one with his nose always to the ground. If you want a dog that excels at retrieving, whether for hunting or playing fetch or Frisbee, look for the one that's always carrying something in his mouth or enjoys running after a toy.

If conformation showing is something you'd like to get into, the puppy you choose must not only have appropriate physical characteristics, suggesting that at maturity she'll be an excellent example of the breed, but also a personality with pizzazz, to garner attention in the ring. Naturally, desirable physical characteristics are going to vary from breed to breed, but in most cases you'll look for such things as dark eyes, correct ear set, bite, color and coat type. The breeder should be your mentor in this selection process because the puppy you show is going to reflect on his breeding program.

Pet Quality Versus Show Quality

Showing may not be of interest to you, though, and that's okay. A dog's best and highest purpose is to be a companion. When all you want is a best friend, the breeder may suggest that you take a pet-quality puppy.

The term pet quality doesn't mean inferior. In most cases it's a puppy that simply doesn't have the qualities of a show dog. Her ears might not sit quite right on her head, her eyes might be a little too light, or her markings might not be just right. Whatever the case, a pet-quality puppy can be a perfectly good buy. She comes from the same health-checked, temperament-tested parents as a show-quality puppy and has had the same good nutrition and veterinary care.

Whether or not your puppies are "show quality," they will still be devoted companions. (Australian Shepherds)

Temperament Tests

Puppy testing, or temperament testing, is an assessment of a puppy's response to certain stimuli or situations and is used to predict such things as a pup's level of dominance, how trainable she is, whether she has good retrieving ability, whether she's shy or outgoing, and whether she's attracted to people. Temperament tests aren't guaranteed to be accurate, and there's no standardized version of them, but they're easy to do and can help you get an idea of a pup's personality. Puppy testing combined with the breeder's observations can lead you to the best pup for you. With the breeder's permission, you can try the following tests with the puppies you look at.

First, simply watch the puppies to see how they interact with each other. Is there one that dominates the others, or one that stands off to the side, not playing with the others? Either of these pups could have a dominant personality, or one could be dominant and the other shy. To see which applies, clap your hands and call the puppies to you. Some will come running, some will check you out first, then saunter over, and one might shy away, avoiding you altogether. The first two responses indicate puppies that are confident, or cautious but willing, but the latter response is made by a puppy that's frightened of people, not a good sign for a potential pet. A puppy that's shy or fearful isn't easy to raise and may never outgrow the behavior. Don't buy her just because you feel sorry for her.

Walk away from the puppies and see if any of them follow you. Willingness to follow signals a pup that likes people and is interested in them.

Roll or throw a ball or toy, and see which puppies run after it. Award bonus points if one of them brings it back.

One by one, pick the puppies up and gauge their response to being held. Some will squirm, then settle down, while others will continue to struggle to get away. The pup that settles down quickly is more likely to be amenable to training and to be an affectionate pet that is focused on you. Walk away from the other puppies and see if her attitude changes once she's separated from her littermates. A seemingly

There are tests you can perform to judge the personalities of puppies in a litter. (Petit Basset Griffon Vendeen)

shy puppy may open up once she's away from the crowd, and a more confident puppy may become somewhat alarmed at suddenly being taken away from the gang. Keep in mind, however, that the responses to this test can vary depending

on whether you interrupted a fun game or the pup has just woken up from a nap or some other factor.

109

Buying a Puppy Long-Distance

Although meeting a breeder and seeing puppies in person is ideal, it can't always be done, especially if you're looking for a rare breed that isn't available on every street corner. If you find a breeder you like, but he lives across the country, the two of you can screen each other by phone, mail and e-mail. The breeder may be able to send you copies of health certifications, and photos or videos of pups and parents, or can direct you to his Web site where pictures and information are available. If you have a friend or relative in the area, she may be able to visit the breeder's home for you and give you a report. The breeder may ask one of his friends or relatives to do the same at your end. Ask for references from other puppy buyers, just as you would from any other breeder.

Before you buy, discuss guarantees and return policies. A reputable breeder will send a puppy on approval, with a 48-hour, no-questions-asked return policy for a full refund. This gives you time to meet the puppy, take her to your veterinarian for a checkup, and decide if she's really what you want. Again, don't accept a puppy that is younger than 7 weeks.

Most breeders are experienced at shipping and will try to send the puppy on a nonstop flight at a time of day when she won't be subject to excessive temperatures. Be aware that some airlines have a moratorium on shipping dogs during the summer, when temperatures can soar.

Whether you buy long-distance or from a local breeder, don't feel obliged to buy from the first litter you investigate. The more litters you look at, and the more mature dogs of the breed you meet, the better picture you will get of the breed and the more knowledgeable you will become about choosing just the right pup for you.

chapter 8

Contracts
and **Other**
Paperwork

There's a lot of paperwork involved in buying a puppy: a sales contract, registration papers, the puppy's pedigree and guidelines from the breeder. Here's what you need to know about what all those papers mean—or don't mean.

(American Pit Bull Terrier)

Sales Contract

Many breeders ask puppy buyers to sign a sales or purchase contract. Such a contract usually covers the rights of buyer and seller, any health guarantees, buyback or return policies, spay/neuter requirements, and delivery of registration papers, which are sometimes withheld until the breeder has proof that the pup has been spayed or neutered. Some breeders keep puppies on co-ownerships, meaning that they have a say in whether the puppy is bred or shown, for instance. Others co-own the dog only until she's spayed and then transfer complete ownership to the buyer. Some contracts contain clauses requiring that the dog be returned to the breeder if there's ever a reason the buyer can't keep her. Most sales contracts are fairly simple and straightforward. Be sure you read the contract and understand everything in it before you sign. Puppy sales contracts are legally binding, and either buyer or seller may go to court to enforce it.

Registration Papers

What does it mean when we say that a dog has papers? The term "papers" refers not to the newspapers used in potty training but to a dog's registration papers. The fact that a puppy or dog is registered simply means that her parents were registered members of the same breed. A connotation of quality often goes along with the terms "registered," "purebred" or "papered," but registration papers are only as good as the breeder behind them. Any dog can be registered, even if she's born blind, with three legs or with some hereditary defect, as long as her parents were registered. AKC papers, or papers from any other registry, don't guarantee quality, only lineage.

If a dog "has papers," it simply means that her parents were registered members of the same breed. (Shih Tzus)

Your registered puppy will come with what's known as a blue slip, or AKC registration form, already filled out by the breeder with the puppy's breed, sex, color, date of birth, the registered names of her parents and the breeder's name. All you have to do is complete the form with your name and address, as well as the name under which you plan to register the dog. Send the blue slip to the AKC with the appropriate fee. Once the form is processed, you'll be mailed a registration certificate, which you can frame, put in your dog's puppy book, or toss in a drawer.

If your puppy is pet quality, the breeder may give her limited registration. This means that your puppy will be registered and have papers, but if she produces off-spring, those puppies will not be able to be registered. Dogs with limited registration can't be shown in con-formation classes, but they can compete in perfor-mance events such as obedience trials, agility and tracking. Limited registration is a way for breeders to withhold judgment on a puppy that may or may not

A pedigree is simply a canine family tree, showing your precious puppy's ances-tors for several generations. (West Highland White Terrier)

have show or breeding potential. If the puppy you buy turns out to have star quality and you and the breeder agree that she should be shown or bred, the limited registra-tion can then be changed to a full registration.

Pedigree

Like a family tree, a pedi-gree is a written record of a dog's ancestry for three or more genera-tions. The names of dogs with conformation, obedience or working titles are often boldfaced or highlighted in red. A pedigree may also indicate health certifications and colors. The breeder can explain to you how to read it.

Like registration papers, a pedigree is nice to have if you want to show off your pup's heritage, but it's not really an important or necessary document unless you plan to breed your dog. Then you'll want to study the pedigree carefully—ideally, under the tutelage of the breeder—to learn more about the dogs in your pup's background, such as their good qualities, faults, any health problems they may bring to the table and longevity.

Health and Care

Probably the most important paperwork you'll receive from the breeder are your puppy's vaccination and deworming records, as well as the results of any tests for hereditary disorders. Take these to your veterinarian when your pup goes in for his checkup. They'll become part of her permanent record.

Your dog's health records may be the most important canine paperwork you have. (Cocker Spaniel)

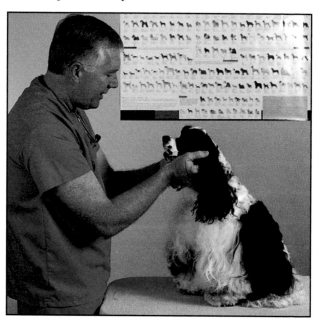

Most breeders also put together puppy packets to guide you in those first few days or weeks of puppy ownership. A puppy packet can be as simple as a page of tips on feeding and housetraining or as elaborate as a folder containing your puppy's picture and pedigree; a brief history of the breed; information about the pup's sire and dam; advice on nutrition, grooming, housetraining and obedience training;

and a copy of the sales contract. He may also include a recommended reading list, a club membership application, and a copy of the breed standard. If you're acquiring an older dog, the packet may include a Canine Good Citizen certificate or obedience class graduation certificate. You'll want to read everything in the packet to make sure you and your pup get off to a good start together, but don't hesitate to call the breeder if you have questions. A good one will be more than happy to help and advise you throughout your dog's life.

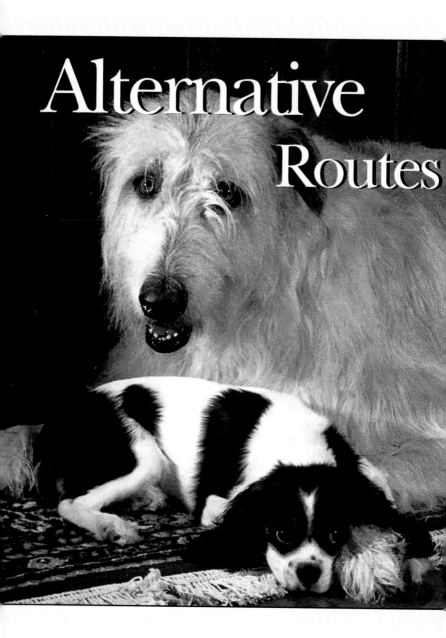

Alternative Routes

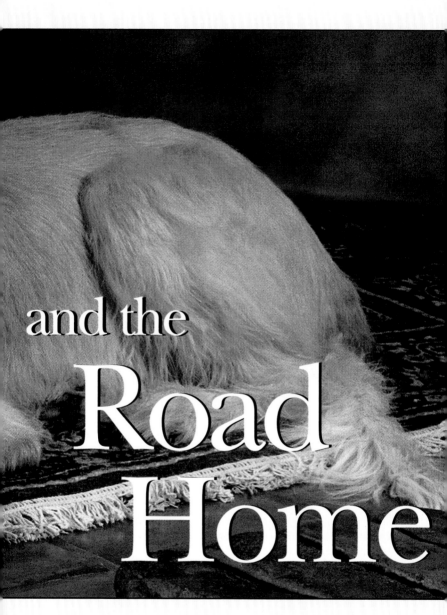

and the
Road
Home

Where to Find Your Dog

(Dalmatians)

Breed Rescue Groups

Purebred dogs may end up with breed rescue groups because their people are moving and can't or won't take them along, their owners divorce, die or become ill and can't care for them, or their owners weren't prepared for the responsibilities of dog ownership. If you would like to own a purebred dog but feel guilty about spending a lot of money on a pet when there are so many homeless dogs in the world, breed rescue is a good compromise.

BREED CLUBS

Most breed clubs operate rescue groups to care for homeless members of their breed. They foster the dogs until they can be placed, screen potential adopters, and raise funds to care for rescued dogs through activities such as auctions and donations. Not surprisingly, popular breeds such as Cocker Spaniels and Labrador Retrievers are frequently in need of rescue, but even rare breeds can find themselves in need of a new home.

Dogs adopted from breed rescue groups are usually adults, but puppies are occasionally available. You shouldn't count on getting a puppy unless you're prepared for a long wait.

What to Expect

Breed rescue groups typically screen adopters just as carefully as breeders screen puppy buyers. Since these dogs have already lost their homes at least once, rescue coordinators want to make sure they go to appropriate homes so that they don't keep going through the rescue/adoption cycle. Expect the rescue group to require the dog to be spayed or neutered or to have already neutered the dog before placing it. In return, you'll most likely get a dog that's up-to-date on his vaccinations and deworming. Some clubs with large budgets do extensive physical rehabilitation, grooming heavily matted or filthy coats, cleaning a dog's teeth or treating him for heartworms, for instance, before placing him.

Adoption fees support rescue efforts and are usually based on the amount of money paid for veterinary costs associated with preparing the dog for adoption, such as a veterinary exam, vaccinations, or spay/neuter surgery. Some clubs establish a minimum amount to ensure their ability to help animals that need more of a financial investment than will be recouped through adoption. Adoption fees can go up to $150 or more, but you get a lot for your money, and it goes toward helping other dogs that need homes.

If you're patient with the process and willing to ask as many questions as you're asked, the adoption should go smoothly. The time you take is well worth it to make sure you and the dog are happy with each other.

A Typical Adoption Process

Each rescue group has its own procedures, but in general you can expect to be educated about the breed and questioned thoroughly about your ability to provide a home for this particular type of dog. They'll want to be sure you understand the breed's unique characteristics and requirements, temperament and potential health problems, as well as the individual dog's background and level of training, if any. Some rescue dogs have special needs, and the person interviewing you will want to make sure you're as close a match as possible. The reason so many dogs are placed with rescue groups is because their former owners didn't ask enough questions of themselves or about dog ownership before they got the breed. If you've read this far, you are already familiar with those questions and are prepared to give a dog a safe, loving home for life.

Successful rescues make everyone happy! (Pembroke Welsh Corgi)

QUESTIONS YOU'LL BE ASKED

Your answers to these questions will help you and the interviewer decide if you're ready for dog ownership and if a rescue dog is right for you. You may have already thought through some or all of these questions, and some may not apply to you and the dog you're thinking about adopting. Many people find the questions helpful, though, in thinking through their decision about adopting a dog and in preparing for it. You may be asked these questions in person, by telephone, e-mail, or the club may ask you to fill out an application, which will then be reviewed.

Family Members

Who will be the dog's primary caretaker, responsible for feeding, training and exercise?

Does everyone in the household want a dog, or just the children?

Are any family members allergic to or uncomfortable around dogs?

Are there small children in the household, or who visit frequently? How old are they, and have they had experience with dogs? Toy breeds aren't usually suited to household with small children, or with children who want a dog they can play touch football with.

Are you prepared for a long-term commitment to the dog?

Other Pets

What has been your experience with dogs and other pets? If you've had other animals, what has happened to them?

If you currently have other dogs or pets, what are their breeds/sizes/ages, and what are they like with other animals?

Do you have the time and energy to care for another dog?

Have you had experience with this or similar breeds?

If you have large dogs, would they be likely to injure this breed? If the answer is yes, are you able to manage a multi-dog household by supervising and segregating the dogs as needed to prevent injury?

Training

What are your plans for training the dog? Training classes? Private, at-home trainer? Training the dog yourself from prior experience or from reading a book?

Have you ever successfully house-trained a dog? How do you plan to accomplish housetraining?

Dogs are very trainable, but they don't respond well to harsh methods or corrections. Are you familiar with and willing to use positive training techniques?

A rescue team may ask you questions about your prior experience with animals. (Labrador Retriever)

Temperament

What attracts you to this breed's personality/behavior?

Are there behaviors that you can't tolerate in a dog?

Do you prefer dogs that are easygoing or feisty? Energetic or couch potatoes? Affectionate and outgoing toward everyone or reserved with strangers?

Do you have the time, experience and desire to work with a dog that needs special help with training or socialization, if one is available for adoption?

Is there anything you've experienced with previous dogs, or seen in other people's dogs, that you especially do or don't want in your adoptive dog?

Practicalities

Will the dog spend most of his time indoors or outdoors?

Where will he sleep?

Where will he be during the day when people are around?

Where will he be when family members are at work or school?

How much time every day will the dog be alone?

Will someone have the time and commitment to provide enough exercise and potty breaks? Play and petting time? Training time?

Are you financially prepared to provide a dog with good-quality food, veterinary care, training, and everything else a dog needs, especially if you're adopting a large breed?

Housing

Do you own or rent your home? If you rent, does your landlord permit pets?

Does your housing situation allow you to safely and legally keep a dog?

Does your city, homeowners association or apartment complex limit the number or size of pets you can have?

Do you know if your locality has such a limit, and if so, will the addition of a new dog allow you to stay within that limit?

Do you have a securely fenced yard? If not, will you be able to take your dog outside on lead for potty breaks and exercise?

If your house has areas in which an unsupervised dog could do harm to himself or your possessions, will you be able to confine him to safe areas when he can't be supervised?

You'll want to ask your own questions as well, about the dog's history, health, and behavior in the foster home to ensure that you can give him a suitable environment and the necessary behavioral structure. Ask why the dog was given up. If he was given away because he didn't like children, he's probably not going to do any better with your children. But if he simply had behavioral problems such as barking or chewing, you may be able to resolve those through training.

REFERENCES

You will probably be asked for references from people who can attest to your willingness and ability to give a dog appropriate medical care, exercise, nutrition, and love. If you've had a dog or other pet before, your veterinarian should be one of these references. Other references might come from a groomer or dog trainer (if you've previously owned a pet), a friend or neighbor who breeds or shows dogs, or your landlord.

You may need to provide references to a rescue group to show that you are a responsible and capable person. Rescue groups strive to place dogs with dependable new owners so that the dog in question will never need to be rescued again. (Australian Cattle Dog)

HOME VISIT

If your application is suitable and your references are good, the next step is a home visit and an opportunity to meet a prospective adoptee. Set up a time that's convenient for you and the interviewer. Meeting in person gives all of you a chance to ask further questions and allows the interviewer to make sure that your home situation is appropriate. Don't feel as if your home has to be spotless before the interview. Rescue placement volunteers are people, too, and their homes are likely covered with dog hair, toys and other signs of canine life. They're more concerned with the reaction between you and the dog than with your housekeeping skills.

If all goes well, you'll just need to sign the adoption contract to become the happy owner of a loving rescue dog. Most such contracts require the adopting family to provide proper care—spelled out in the document—and to return the dog to the rescue group if they're ever unable to keep him.

To find a breed rescue group, contact the national breed club or see the listings under Web sites in chapter 11.

Pet Stores

Many people buy dogs from pet stores, either on impulse or because they're unaware of other sources for purebred dogs. While a pet shop puppy may tug at the heartstrings, you should hold a pet store to the same high standards that you would expect a reputable breeder to meet. After all, you're spending a lot of money for a dog, and you should expect full value from your purchase. A puppy from a pet store costs as much or more than it would from a breeder, so there's no reason not to demand the same quality of health and temperament.

Veterinarians often advise their clients against purchasing dogs from pet stores because of bad experiences with the dogs' health. With this in mind, ask to see the appropriate health certifications for the breed you're interested in. For a German Shepherd Dog, for instance, the pet store should be able to show Orthopedic Foundation for Animals (OFA) good or better ratings for both parents; for a Poodle or Cocker Spaniel, Canine Eye Registry Foundation (CERF) approvals for both parents. Ask a veterinarian in advance what health problems you should be concerned about in a particular breed and what certifications the parents should have. Look in the resources section in chapter 11 for contact information for health registries and do your research.

Just as you would if you were interviewing a breeder, walk away from stores that claim that a particular breed or line doesn't have any health problems. All breeds have some type of hereditary health problem, but responsible breeders work hard to keep the incidence low in their lines.

Does the store offer a written health guarantee? At a minimum, a health guarantee should be good for 30 days. A better guarantee lasts for one year. Immediately after purchase, take the dog to a veterinarian for a thorough exam. You don't want to wait until your family is attached to the puppy before finding out that it has a health problem. This is also true for a dog purchased directly from a breeder.

Ask where the store acquires its puppies. Young puppies that are shipped long distances are stressed and more susceptible to illness. Commercial suppliers often keep dogs in crowded conditions, which also increases the likelihood of disease.

Ideally, someone who produces puppies belongs to a breed club and exhibits his or her dogs to determine their quality. Does the pet store's supplier meet this qualification? Are photos of the parents available? Ask if the puppy's parents are AKC titled. And be aware that the by-laws of most breed clubs prohibit members from selling dogs through third parties such as pet stores or brokers.

If the pet store is selling mixed-breed puppies, don't be misled by a fancy name or "registration" from an organization other than the American Kennel Club or the United Kennel Club. Schnoodles, Cockapoos, Lhasapoos and so on are not recognized breeds, and there's no reason to pay hundreds of dollars for such a mix.

Temperament is important as well. Without seeing the parents in person, it's difficult to know what a puppy's personality will be like. Ask if the parents have been temperament tested (they'll have a TT after their names). Also keep in mind that puppies from pet stores can be more difficult to housetrain because they're allowed to eliminate in their cages. Once this habit is ingrained, it makes crate-training almost impossible.

The best way to acquire a dog from a pet store is through adoption from a sponsoring humane society or group. Some stores don't sell dogs themselves but work in tandem with animal shelters or purebred rescue groups. They host adoption events or provide off-site facilities for these organizations. Finding a dog this way is a win-win situation for all involved. It's convenient for the adopter who might otherwise avoid the shelter for fear of being overwhelmed, it provides business for the store, the organization places a dog and the dog finds a loving home.

Adopting from a Shelter

Dogs end up in shelters for many reasons: because their people didn't realize how much work a dog would be, are moving to a new place that doesn't allow pets, or because divorce or death breaks up the home. For these and other reasons, there's a never-ending supply of dogs at animal shelters. They come in all shapes, sizes, ages and types. Many are mixed breeds, but sometimes popular purebred dogs—and even some that aren't so popular—are available at animal shelters. You may not find a purebred on your first trip there, but some shelters keep waiting lists of people interested in specific breeds.

Popular purebred dogs are sometimes available at animal shelters. (Basset Hound)

When you go to a shelter, it's a good idea to have a preconceived notion of what you're looking for in a dog

127

so you won't be overwhelmed by the numbers. Do you want a dog with a long or short coat, or one of a specific color? Make a list of the qualities you want so you won't become distracted when you're looking.

A FAMILY DECISION

A good way to make the selection is for the whole family to go through the shelter together. Make three sweeps of the facility. On the first go-round, just enjoy looking at all the dogs. Don't try to make a decision yet. Walk through again. This time, each person should choose two dogs he or she would like to adopt. The third time through, look at each dog chosen, comparing him to the list to see if he meets the criteria. Eliminate those that don't. Take the list of remaining dogs to a shelter employee and ask for more information about them.

*Adopting from
a shelter means
saving a life.
(Doberman
Pinscher)*

It's rare that you'll be making a completely blind decision when you choose a dog from a shelter. Shelter personnel see the dogs on a regular basis and can give you insight into each dog's personality and habits. If a dog was turned in by her owner, the shelter may have detailed information about her health and personality, such as whether she's spayed, likes children, prefers men or women, has any training, or chases cats.

In the best of all worlds, the home situation you can offer will be similar to what the dog is already used to. For instance, older dogs may have a tough time fitting into a home with very young children unless they came from a family with children. Once you've discussed your choices with shelter personnel, you can meet with the dog or dogs left on the list to make your decision.

WHAT TO EXPECT

Remember that a dog in a shelter is in an unnatural situation. She's likely to be stressed and frightened and may not show to best advantage. Ask if you can take the dog out on a leash or into a visiting room so you can get to know each other on a one-on-one basis. A dog that shies away in the kennel area may loosen up once she's in a less stressful situation. Spend as much time as possible becoming acquainted with the dogs you look at so you can be sure you're making the right decision.

The Adoption Process

When you've finally found the perfect dog, you'll probably be asked to fill out an application and meet with an adoption counselor to discuss the particular needs of the dog you've chosen and how she'll fit into your home situation. Some shelters ask that all family members be present at this interview to make sure everyone's in favor of getting a dog. As part of the application, the shelter may require you to show picture identification or something that shows your current address. If

> ### THE OLDER DOG
>
> Don't pass up a dog because of his advanced age. Adopting an older dog can be a wonderful experience. He may not be around as long as a younger dog, but the rewards of ownership can outweigh the eventual loss. It's natural to be reluctant to become attached to an older dog, but death is a part of life, and the unconditional love of an older dog far outweighs the pain of eventually losing him. People who adopt an older dog from a municipal shelter can take great pride and pleasure in knowing that they've saved a life.

you rent rather than own your home, shelter personnel may contact your landlord to make sure pets are permitted. If you've owned pets previously or currently have other pets, a letter from your veterinarian stating that you've been responsible pet owners can also come in handy.

While some shelters permit same-day adoptions, others ask that you wait 24 hours to think over the decision. In the meantime, your paperwork will be processed and your dog will be readied for a home visit. If all goes well, the adoption will be approved. Like breeders and breed rescue groups, shelter personnel want to make sure that the dogs they place are going to appropriate homes where they'll be happy, so don't be offended by the need for paperwork and interviews.

You will need to pay an adoption fee before you take home your new dog. (Labrador Retriever)

ADOPTION FEES

If you're approved for the adoption, the shelter will probably charge a fee of $25 or more. Many times, this fee includes spay/neuter surgery, vaccinations, deworming and sometimes other veterinary treatments. That's a pretty good deal for a new best friend.

Some shelters offer training classes for new dog owners to help smooth the dog's introduction into the family. Try to have the whole family attend so you can all learn how to communicate and interact with your new dog. Shelter personnel may stay in touch with you for the first few weeks to make sure all is going well. Give them a call if you have questions about behavior or care. There may be a trainer or behaviorist on staff who can help.

Adoption is an opportunity to make a difference in a dog's life, and you will find that your good deed brings returns many times over in the love and companionship the dog gives you.

chapter

Bringing Your Dog Home

Whether you're buying a puppy or adopting a dog from a breed rescue group or animal shelter, you'll want to make sure your new friend is comfortable in your home. That means bringing him home at the appropriate age, having the right equipment on hand to care for him, and successfully introducing him to other pets.

Supplies You'll Need

To fill up the time before your dog comes to live with you, go on a shopping spree at a pet supply store. Your dog will need food and water dishes; a high-quality dog food; a collar, leash and tag; a crate; a mat or other bedding to go inside the crate; grooming tools; toys; and a box of treats.

A breeder will probably send you home with a two- or three-day supply of the food your new puppy is used to eating. If you plan to continue feeding that food, buy another bag of it. If you want to switch to something else, gradually mix in the new food with the old over a period of a week to prevent diarrhea or other digestive problems.

Order an ID tag with your name and phone number on it. Some stores have machines now that will engrave tags instantly. When you pick up your dog, put the collar and tag on him before you walk out of the breeder's house or shelter.

ALL ABOUT CRATES

A crate is something no new dog owner should be without. It serves as a dog's bed, as a safe place of confinement when you're not around to keep an eye on him, and is an excellent housetraining tool because

most dogs are reluctant to soil their sleeping areas. Dogs feel secure in crates and often go to them when they want to take a nap or escape from the kids. The crate should be the dog's refuge, where he can't be bothered, so don't let the kids climb on it, or poke their fingers inside or crawl inside with the dog.

Most crates are made of molded plastic or wire.

A crate is your dog's private escape from the sometimes hectic pace of human life. (Beagle)

Some new models made of heavyweight packcloth or other water-resistant materials are available, but these are best used for traveling and aren't recommended for puppies or dogs that like to chew or dig. A molded plastic crate, or airline-style crate, is sturdy, easy to clean, and offers the dog privacy. Wire crates give better ventilation and can be covered for privacy. Some fold up for easy storage. The type of crate you choose depends on your preference as well as what you plan to do with your dog. If you'll be shipping him at some point—to dog shows or because you're moving—he'll need an airline crate.

GROOMING TOOLS AND SUPPLIES

The grooming tools you'll need depend on the type of dog you get. Brushes come in different sizes so you can get one to fit your dog. You can use a brush with natural or nylon bristles for a dog with a short, medium or long coat. A pin brush with long stainless steel or plastic bristles—which resemble pins—is good for long-haired dogs because it won't break the coat. A hound mitt, which has short, nubby bristles, usually made of rubber, is great for removing dead hair and shining the coat of a shorthaired dog. A wire slicker brush removes dead hair and mats and can be used on dogs with medium or long coats.

Guillotine-style clippers will keep your dog's nails from getting too long. Clip nails regularly so that the quick doesn't grow long and make the nail painful to cut. Just in case you do "quick" the dog and cause the nail to bleed, have some styptic powder on hand as well to stop the bleeding. Dog nail clippers and styptic powder are available at pet supply stores.

Nail clipping is an important and surprisingly easy process.

Choose a mild shampoo formulated for dogs and safe for use on puppies. A mild shampoo that doesn't contain flea- or tick-killing pesticides can be used as often as weekly, but you don't have to bathe your dog that often unless you want to. Most dogs that are kept well brushed and groomed don't develop a heavy doggy odor and need baths only when they get dirty.

133

Don't forget a doggy toothbrush and toothpaste. If you start brushing your pup's teeth now and get him used to it, he'll be less likely to develop that ugly brown plaque on his teeth that makes his breath stinky.

Pick out a few toys for your dog as well. Good choices include hard rubber toys, rope bones and tennis ball toys. Any toy you choose should be large enough that it can't be swallowed. Avoid toys with bells, buttons or other pieces that could be easily chewed off and swallowed.

Last but not least, buy a box of puppy-size treats. As soon as you get him, you can start teaching your dog simple commands such as sit and come, and luring him with a treat will make the process lots of fun for both of you. Hard biscuits are a good choice because they'll help keep your dog's teeth clean.

Toys can make life worth living! (Pembroke Welsh Corgi)

Introducing Other Pets

Before marriage, couples often undergo counseling to ensure that their personalities and lifestyles will be compatible and to help them deal effectively with conflicts. Bringing a new pet into a household entails many of the same concerns, albeit on a different level. While we can't exactly sit down with all our animals to talk out their potential problems, we can take steps to keep tensions to a minimum and develop cordial relationships.

Begin by making formal introductions. This is not the time to just throw everyone together and hope for the best. That sometimes works at cocktail parties, but animals tend to prefer more ritual and structure in their lives. Take it slow, and consider everyone's personalities. The introduction technique you use depends on which animals are involved.

DOGS

If you have another dog, consider introducing the two someplace other than your home. When dogs are on neutral territory, such as a park or a friend's house, they're less likely to display territorial behaviors that could cause an argument between them. With both dogs on a leash (have a friend or other family member hold the new dog's leash), let them go through the traditional canine greeting ritual: sniffing each other from head to tail. If they seem to get along, let them play a while and get used to each other. Usually, dogs do best in opposite-sex pairs, so hopefully you've considered this when making your selection. Two males or two females will be more likely to disagree or to spar for the position of top dog.

Once you take the dogs home, make sure each one has his own bed, dishes, toys and other items. This will reduce the chance that they'll get into arguments over who gets to play with the Kong toy or who gets to sleep where. Dog kindergarten doesn't really address the concept of sharing, and you shouldn't expect your dogs to abide by this type of human construct. What's "fair" or "right" in human terms means nothing to dogs. Be sure you give your first dog some extra-special attention so he doesn't feel as if he's being ignored.

CATS

Cats are another matter altogether. If your cat is already used to dogs, the introduction should go smoothly, depending on the new dog's manners. Bring him in on a leash so you can control any interaction between the two. Your cat may hiss or swipe at him, just to let him know who's boss. This is understandable, but you'll want to protect the dog from being injured by her claws. Never hold a cat out to a dog, especially a large one. He may use the opportunity to try to take a hunk out of her.

If dogs are a new experience for your cat, she may go into hiding for a few hours or even a few days. Don't try to drag her out and make her interact with the dog. She'll do best if she can get used to his scent and presence over a period of time, on her own terms. Until they get to know and accept one another, be sure the dog is confined or otherwise separated from the cat when you can't be around to supervise.

Close human supervision is a must when cats and dogs meet. (American Pit Bull Terrier)

SMALL ANIMALS

Before presenting your new dog to a small pet such as a ferret, guinea pig, rabbit, mouse or rat, make sure the small animal is securely caged. Under your watchful eye, let the dog sniff at the cage and get a good look at the occupant. That opportunity to sniff is important to all animals who are far more reliant on their senses of smell than we are. Your presence ensures that the dog knows that this new animal is there with your knowledge and consent rather than being a wild animal to be caught. This also allows the dog to examine the animal without feeling as if he has to sneak around to look at it.

Even if everyone seems to get along, limited interaction is best for small rodents or other preylike pets. This may include letting them roam the sofa or floor while you watch television, keeping a close eye on everyone, of course. With the best of intentions, a dog can inadvertently hurt a small playmate with rough play. Even little dogs are big enough that they can hurt a small animal by stepping on it.

Not every pet combination is a marriage made in heaven, but in most cases you can look forward to a peaceful coexistence among your animal friends.

The First Day and Night

Keep things low key for your puppy's first day. He's still just a baby, so let him explore and get settled in at his own pace. Limit his introductions to family members for now; you don't want to overwhelm him by inviting over all the neighbors. They can meet him later, one or two at a time, once he's more familiar with you and your home.

It's essential that you take a long weekend or even a week to get the dog used to his

Your new little bundle of fur may be a bit bewildered at first, so give her plenty of time to explore her new environs. (Golden Retriever)

new surroundings. You'll want to start him on a feeding and elimination schedule to make housetraining easier. If he's still a puppy, take him out to potty as soon as you hear him awaken in the morning, after every meal, and after naps and playtime. And don't just throw him out in the backyard to do his business; put a leash on him and go out with him. When he eliminates, put a name to the action—"Go potty"—

137

and praise him—"Good puppy to go potty." By taking him out on a leash and praising him, you give him the idea that he's out there for a purpose. For that reason, don't combine play time and potty time. Keep them separate so you can get him in the habit of going whenever you take him out on a leash.

WHINING AND CRYING

Your dog will probably be lonesome that first night—especially if he's a puppy. He's used to sleeping in a pile with his mom and littermates, after all. It's a good idea to put his crate in your bedroom. If he sleeps in there, he won't be as lonely and will start the bonding process with you. The puppy may whine or cry at first. If he does this, don't go comfort him or let him into the bed with you. That just lets him know that crying gets a good response from you (puppies are smart and learn these things very quickly).

New adult dogs need a little extra TLC in new homes just as much as puppies do. (Jack Russell Terrier)

He'll quiet down soon enough, especially if you've put a cuddly toy in the crate with him or left him with a biscuit for the night.

Most of this advice applies to older dogs as well. Let them explore the house, play with them if they want to, but mostly just let them get to know you. You don't need to take an adult dog out to potty as frequently as you do a puppy, but it's still a good idea to get him used to your schedule so he knows when he'll be able to go out. Sleeping in a crate in your room will accustom him to your scent and make him feel more at home.

You've just entered into one of the greatest relation-ships there is: human and dog. Love, enjoy and care for your new companion, and he'll give you untold pleasure over the years.

part five

Beyond the Basics

chapter 11

Resources

Breed Registries

Registry organizations register purebred dogs. The American Kennel Club is the oldest and largest in this country, and currently recognizes over 145 breeds. The United Kennel Club registers some breeds the AKC doesn't (including the American Pit Bull Terrier and the Miniature Fox Terrier), as well as many of the same breeds. The others included here are for your reference; the AKC can provide you with a list of foreign registries.

Every breed recognized by the American Kennel Club has a national (parent) club. National clubs are a great source of information on your dog's breed. You can get the name of the secretary of the club by contacting:

American Kennel Club (AKC)
5580 Centerview Dr., Suite 250
Raleigh, NC 27606-3389
(919) 233-9767
www.akc.org

United Kennel Club (UKC)
100 E. Kilgore Road
Portage, MI 49002-5584
(616) 343-9020
www.ukcdogs.com

American Dog Breeders Assn.
P.O. Box 1771
Salt Lake City, UT 84110
(801) 936-7513
http://members.aol.com/bstofshw
(Registers American Pit Bull Terriers)

American Rare Breed Association
9921 Frank Tippet Road
Cheltenham, MD 20612
(301) 868-5718
www.arba.org

Canadian Kennel Club
89 Skyway Avenue
Etobicoke, Ontario
Canada M9W 6R4
(800) 250-8040
(416) 675-5511
www.ckc.ca

Health Registries

Canine Health Foundation
251 West Garfield Road, Suite 160
Aurora, OH 44202
(330) 995-0807
www.akcchf.org

Canine Eye Registry Foundation (CERF)
Department of Veterinary Clinical Science
School of Veterinary Medicine
Purdue University
West Lafayette, IN 47907
(765) 794-4600
http://vet.purdue.edu

Orthopedic Foundation for Animals (OFA)
2300 E. Nifong Blvd.
Columbia, MO 65201-3856
(573) 442-0418; Fax, (573) 875-5073
e-mail: ofa@offa.org
www.offa.org

Books

GENERAL

American Kennel Club. *The Complete Dog Book*, 19th Ed. *Rev.* New York: Howell Book House, 1998.

Rogers Clark, Anne and Brace, Andrew H. *The International Encyclopedia of Dogs*. New York: Howell Book House, 1995.

Carlson, Liisa, DVM, and James Giffin, MD. *Dog Owner's Home Veterinary Handbook*. New York: Howell Book House, 1999.

DeBitetto, James, DVM, and Hodgson, Sarah. *You & Your Puppy: Training & Health Care For Puppy's First Year*. New York: Howell Book House, 2000.

Spadafori, Gina. *Dogs For Dummies*, 2nd Ed. New York: IDG Books Worldwide, Inc., 2000.

ABOUT TRAINING

Arden, Andrea. *Dog-Friendly Dog Training*. New York: Howell Book House, 1999.

Benjamin, Carol Lea. *Dog Training in 10 Minutes*. New York:Howell Book House, 1997.

Dunbar, Ian, PhD, MRCVS. *How to Teach a New Dog Old Tricks*, James & Kenneth Publishers, 1998. Order from the publisher at 2140 Shattuck Ave. #2406, Berkeley, CA 94704. (510) 658-8588.

Evans, Job Michael. *People, Pooches and Problems*. New York: Howell Book House, 2001.

Hodgson, Sarah. *Dog Tricks For Dummies*. New York: IDG Books Worldwide, Inc., 2000.

ABOUT ACTIVITIES

American Rescue Dog Association. *Search and Rescue Dogs*. New York: Howell Book House, 1991.

Burch, Mary. *Volunteering With Your Pet*. New York: Howell Book House, 1996

Hall, Lynn. *Dog Showing for Beginners.* New York: Howell Book House, 1994.

O' Neil, Jacqueline. *All About Agility.* New York: Howell Book House, 1999.

Vollhard, Jack and Wendy. *The Canine Good Citizen.* New York: Howell Book House, 1994.

Magazines

All except the *AKC Gazette & The Bark* are available on newsstands and at pet stores.

The *AKC GAZETTE*, The Official Journal for the Sport of Purebred Dogs.
American Kennel Club
260 Madison Avenue, 4th Floor
New York, NY 10016
www.akc.org

The Bark.
2810 8th Street
Berkeley, CA 94710
www.thebark.com

Dog Fancy
Fancy Publications
3 Burroughs
Irvine, CA 92718
www.animalnetwork.com/dogs/

Dog & Kennel
Pet Publishing, Inc.
7-L Dundas Circle
Greensboro, NC 27407
www.dogandkennel.com

Dog World
Maclean Hunter Publishing Corp.
29 N. Wacker Drive
Chicago, IL 60606
www.dogworldmag.com

Videos

"SIRIUS Puppy Training," by Ian Dunbar, PhD, MRCVS. James & Kenneth Publishers, 2140 Shattuck Ave. #2406, Berkeley, CA 94704. Order from the publisher.

"Training the Companion Dog," from Dr. Dunbar's British TV Series, James & Kenneth Publishers. (See address above).

The American Kennel Club produces videos on every breed of dog, as well as on hunting tests, field trials and other areas of interest to purebred dog owners. For more information, write to AKC/Video Fulfillment, 5580 Centerview Dr., Suite 200, Raleigh, NC 27606.

Activity Clubs

Write these organizations for information on the activities they sponsor.

American Kennel Club (AKC)
260 Madison Avenue, 4th Floor
New York, NY 10016
(212) 696-8200
(Conformation Shows, Obedience Trials, Field Trials and Hunting Tests, Agility, Canine Good Citizen, Lure Coursing, Herding, Tracking, Earthdog Tests, Coonhunting.)

United Kennel Club (UKC)
100 E. Kilgore Road
Portage, MI 49002-5584
(616) 343-9020
ukcdogs.com
(Conformation Shows, Obedience Trials, Agility, Hunting for Various Breeds, Terrier Trials and more.)

North American Flyball Assn.
1400 West Devon Ave., #152
Chicago, IL 60660
www.flyball.org

Trainers

For assistance in locating a trainer near you, contact:

Association of Pet Dog Trainers
66 Morris Avenue, Suite 2A
Springfield, NJ 07081
1 (800) PET-DOGS

American Dog Trainers' Network
161 West 4th Street
New York, NY 10014
(212) 727-7257
www.canine.org

Glossary
of Veterinary
Terminology

Affected   A dog that shows evidence of a disease.

Brachycephalic   Dogs with short noses and flat faces. Brachy-cephalic dogs are more prone to heatstroke than other dogs.

Brucellosis   A sexually transmitted bacterial disease of the genital tract.

Cardiac ultrasound   The use of ultrasonic sound waves to examine the heart. Used to diagnose heart conditions.

Cardiomyopathy   Enlargement of the heart.

Carrier   A dog that can transmit a disease gene to its offspring with-out showing symptoms itself.

Cartilage   Specialized connective tissue that plays a role in bone growth and joint formation.

Castration   Surgical removal of the testes.

Cataract   An opacity of the lens of the eye, which can be any size or shape, single or multiple. Cataracts may be inherited, congenital or acquired.

Congenital   A condition existing at birth.

Copper toxicosis   An inherited condition that occurs when high levels of copper accumulate in the liver, causing liver disease. High incidence occurs in Bedlington Terriers.

Craniomandibular osteopathy (CMO)   A jaw deformity caused by the formation of too much dense bone. Occurs in Scottish Terriers and West Highland White Terriers.

Cryptorchidism   The failure of one or both testicles to descend into the scrotum. Suspected to be hereditary.

Echocardiography   *See* cardiac ultrasound.

Ectropion   Condition in which the eyelid turns outward from the eyeball. Requires surgical correction.

Elbow dysplasia   A malformation of the elbow joint that causes forelimb pain and lameness. Like hip dysplasia, elbow dysplasia is probably caused by multiple factors. It usually requires surgical correction.

Electrocardiogram   An examination of the electrical activity of the heart. Used to diagnose certain heart conditions.

Entropion   A condition in which the eyelid turns inward toward the eyeball. Requires surgical correction.

Epilepsy   A brain disorder that results in seizures, which can be mild or severe. Sometimes controllable with medication.

Genes   Individual units of inheritance that control the transmission of a hereditary characteristic.

Heart murmur   An abnormal heart sound that occurs when blood flows too rapidly or too chaotically through an area of the heart.

Hereditary   A condition transmissible from parent to offspring.

Hip dysplasia   An inherited condition created by multiple factors that occurs when the head of the thigh bone doesn't fit properly in the hip socket, leading to lameness. Severe cases require hip replacement or euthanasia.

Idiopathic   A condition with no known cause.

Mitral valve disease   A backwash of blood through a malfunctioning mitral valve.

Osteochondritis dissecans   A congenital joint problem of the shoulder in which the cartilage is defective, causing pain and lameness. Most common in large, rapidly growing dogs. Requires surgical correction.

Patella   Kneecap.

Patellar luxation   Dislocated kneecap.

Polygenic traits   Traits that stem from the actions of more than one gene.

Progressive retinal atrophy   A family of up to 30 distinct but related eye diseases that cause progressive degeneration of the retina, leading to blindness. Hereditary. No treatment is available.

Pulmonic stenosis   A narrowing of the connection between the right ventricle and the pulmonary artery. A common congenital heart defect.

Radiograph   An x-ray film.

Spay   To surgically remove the ovaries and uterus. Sometimes called an ovariohysterectomy.

Von Willebrand's disease   An inherited bleeding disorder similar to hemophilia. Often misspelled or mispronounced as von Wilderbrand's disease. Reported in German Shepherd Dogs, Golden Retrievers, Doberman Pinschers and Miniature Schnauzers.

Index